Keep on Standing

FROM AFRICAN AFFLUENCE, TO REFUGEE CAMP, TO WORLD ACCLAIMED MUSICIANS

KEEP ON STANDING

THE STORY OF KRYSTAAL

DARLENE POLACHIC

Keep On Standing: The Story of Krystaal

Copyright ©2007 Darlene Polachic
Second Edition 2007
All rights reserved
Printed in Canada
International Standard Book Number: 978-1-894860-37-6

Published by:
Castle Quay Books
1-1295 Wharf Street, Pickering, Ontario, L1W 1A2
Tel: (416) 573-3249   Fax: (416) 981-7922
E-mail: info@castlequaybooks.com
www.castlequaybooks.com

Copy editing by Marina Hofman
Proof reading by Janet Dimond
Cover design by Essence Publishing
Printed at Essence Printing, Belleville, Ontario

Library and Archives Canada Cataloguing in Publication

Polachic, Darlene
    Keep on standing : the story of Krystaal : from African affluence, to refugee camp, to world acclaimed musicians / Darlene Polachic.

ISBN 978-1-894860-37-6

    1. Krystaal (Musical group). 2. Gospel musicians--Canada--Biography. 3. Gospel musicians--Zaire--Biography. I. Title.
ML421.K94P762 2007   782.25'40922   C2007-904759-9

CASTLE QUAY BOOKS

Author's Note

MY VERY FIRST CONTACT WITH THE LWAMBAS CAME SHORTLY AFTER MICHEL and Aliston arrived in Canada, in 1996. Rev. Cal Malena, the pastor of my church, Emmanuel Baptist, in Saskatoon, Saskatchewan, invited Michel to share some of his story with the congregation.

Michel's eyes were still very red and inflamed from the wind-driven sand in the Kenyan refugee camp, where he had lived for five years, and he believed his English was inadequate, but he needn't have worried. The story he told held us all spellbound. I knew right then that I wanted to write the Lwamba brothers' amazing story. I told Michel so at the end of the service. Wisely, I added, "You let me know when you are ready."

Time went on: First Betty came, then Fabian joined the little family group in Saskatoon. The family adjusted to a completely new culture and climate. Krystaal was born and in time began performing at various events and venues with great success and blessing.

One day Michel called me. "We are ready to write that book," he told me. "I have been holding back for a long time. In fact, whenever I saw you in church, I avoided you so you wouldn't remind me about it. But God said very clearly to me, 'Michel, this is not your story. I made you just so you could come to this place and tell other people what I have done so they can know My glory and My power, too. It is time for this story to be told.'"

Michel added, "We know it was God who rescued us and not anything we did ourselves. Our separation and all the things we went through were not easy, but we can see that it was God's purpose for us. We want everyone to know that and to see His glory through the miraculous things He did for us. We can say now that it was all worth it because, in our tribulation, we met Jesus."

Relating their story was not easy. For several months, we met every Tuesday evening and with a tape rolling, Michel, Fabian and Aliston answered my probing questions and dug into painful memories that they had purposely not visited for a long time. We often wept together, as horrifying experiences were relived, cherished memories articulated and God's miraculous fingerprints marvelled at again and again.

The story was first released as *Keep on Standing*, in 2003, but people invariably said, "The book ended too soon. What is Krystaal doing now? We want to know. You must write a sequel."

And indeed, God was using the brothers in such a profound ministry that there was no question the story had to be updated.

This is the result. May Krystaal's ongoing story bless you as much as it blesses me.

Darlene Polachic
Saskatoon, Saskatchewan
2007

Prologue

THE MORNING OF TUESDAY, MAY 9, 1989, DAWNED BLEAK AND COOL IN Lubumbashi, Zaire, which was unusual for that part of east-central Africa. Even though it was still the rainy season, the temperature generally reached around 19° Celsius in early May and the days were sunny and clear.

But this was no ordinary day. Even the weather seemed melancholy, as if Nature was already mourning the horror that was about to take place.

On the University of Lubumbashi campus things were strangely quiet. There were fewer people around than usual; the ones who were present moved about with long faces, their characteristic smiles noticeably absent. They hunched into their heavy jackets against the unseasonable cold.

Michel and Fabian Lwamba knew the sombre atmosphere was about more than just the weather. It was the direct result of a skirmish that had erupted two or three days earlier between university students and the government's special security forces.

The brothers, both political science students at the University of Lubumbashi and leaders of a student political movement with widespread community support, were involved in organizing marches to protest against the blatant injustices being perpetrated against students and staff by Zairean President Mobutu Sese Seko's corrupt and dictatorial government.

Students had discovered that their strategy meetings were being infiltrated by planted "students" who were actually members of the Division Spéciale

Présidentielle (DSP), Mobutu's exclusive and specially trained security force. The plants were also members of Mobutu's own Ngbandi tribe. Their role was to spy on students, report on their plans, and—as would soon be evident—pave the way for a deadly purge that would, once and for all, put an end to the student demonstrations that flagrantly opposed Mobutu's regime.

Only days before, four of the infiltrators were exposed by some students who discovered them communicating on two-way radios. An investigation of their heavily secured lockers revealed a virtual arsenal of high-powered weapons and night-vision equipment.

The four were seized and the university's law department put them on trial and issued a severe punishment. In the meantime, other agents on campus got word to Mobutu about what was happening, and in no time an army helicopter was dispatched to disperse the students and rescue the *mouchards* or cowards, as the informers had come to be known.

In the days since the incident, there were whispers that certain students, those with roots in Mobutu's Ngbandi tribe, were being counselled secretly: "If anyone should say the word *lititi* to you, you must reply, '*Mboka.*'" Only Ngbandis knew what the words meant and among many of them it raised curiosity.

"Why are you telling us this?" a few inquired. "What is going to happen?"

The reply was curt: "Don't ask."

As the day of Tuesday, May 9, unfolded, Michel and Fabian Lwamba grew more and more uneasy. They had noticed military vehicles circling the campus slowly, but the regular army personnel they were used to seeing on the grounds (many of them friends or parents of friends and nearly all residents of Lubumbashi) were curiously absent. In their place were heavily armed strangers with a menacing demeanour and a very different dialect from the local Lingala, the Bantu language spoken throughout much of western Zaire.

The brothers noticed another strange thing. The small building that housed the university's power plant was now ringed by heavily armed guards. As well, the immense gates that gave entrance to the sprawling campus were partially closed. Ordinarily they remained wide open until late in the evening. Today, however, students could come in but no one was allowed to go out.

One student, whose exit from the campus was barred by the armed guards, challenged the action. "Are we prisoners?" he demanded.

"Because of your actions the other day, officials are coming this evening from Kinshasa, the capital, to talk to you. You must be here for that."

The explanation seemed lame. There was something far more sinister in the air than a verbal dressing down. The students could feel it and fear squeezed their hearts.

Almost instinctively, they began to gravitate together in groups to discuss the situation. What would probably happen, they told one another optimistically, was that the national army would come in. "We'll throw a few bottles, exchange a few words and everything will be back to normal again."

At 8:00, the electricity went out.

Across the entire campus there was no power or light. The student dormitories were in darkness. Working and studying for upcoming exams was impossible, so the students opted to remain outside until the lights came back on.

Someone suggested building a bonfire. A number of students ventured into the dense forest that bordered the campus and returned with alarming reports of figures moving stealthily in the darkness. Indeed, as the students looked around them, it appeared the number of soldiers had increased dramatically since the last time they took note.

The crowd of young people, about 400 in number, inched closer to the fire. They pressed in, talking quietly, speculating on the troubling developments, waiting impatiently for the electricity to be restored.

Minutes stretched into hours. Midnight came and went.

Hungry and tired from the long, tension-filled day, many of the students talked about going inside to their rooms.

As the inky darkness deepened over the University of Lubumbashi campus, the crowd around the fire grew thinner. One by one, students drifted away to their dormitory rooms and their beds.

Michel, too, was tired. He had been up since early morning and the thought of sleep was very inviting, but every time he made a move away from the fire, someone else engaged him in conversation.

Suddenly the stragglers around the fire were galvanized by the sound of terrified screams coming from inside the buildings.

"Help! Help!"

Like some macabre, antiphonal chant, the screaming plea could be heard all over the campus.

The killing had begun.

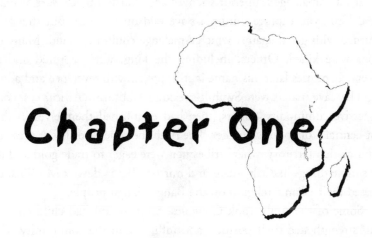

Chapter One

THE LWAMBA CLAN IS PART OF THE BANGU-BANGU TRIBE OF BANTU PEOPLES whose roots are in modern-day Kivu province in the Democratic Republic of Congo (formerly Belgian Congo, Republic of Congo and more recently, Zaire).

The early Bangu-Bangus lived in a part of the country that is intersected by the Luama River, a tributary of the Lualaba, which eventually joins up with the mighty Congo River. The terrain is moderately mountainous with intermittent flat stretches that allowed for cultivation by the early peoples. The area was forested in places with massive oak trees whose wood became one of the country's important exports.

In ancient times, the Bantus were hunters with a secondary occupation of harvesting the rich deposits of gold and diamonds that were present throughout the area. Agricultural endeavours were carried out by the women of the tribe whose responsibility it was to raise the children and cultivate the land for food.

Like most tribes, the early Bangu-Bangus were nomadic, moving on to a new location when food supplies dwindled. Eventually, they began settling for longer periods of time and the day came when they cut down trees and built permanent villages in the clearings. The earth was cultivated and crops sown. A system of authority was established and the men of the tribe spent their spare time fashioning knives and other small weapons for trade.

The Lwamba clan (whose surname means "brave man") rose to tribal pre-eminence among the Bangu-Bangus in the 17th century. The tribe's first king, and the most revered member of the royal line, was Amalenge, a giant of a man, renowned for his physical stature and amazing strength.

It was Amalenge's superior strength and skill as a fierce warrior that initially saved him from capture during a slave raid on the area. But the slave traders returned with guns, against which Amalenge could not stand. Many of his villagers were killed. Others, including the king, were captured and sold into slavery. Centuries later, his name is still spoken with reverence and admiration.

The slave traders were Swahili-speaking Arabs from Africa's east coast. Being aggressive commodity traders, they had established themselves in the area of east-central Congo much earlier. The Arabs became a persistent presence in this resource-rich territory, where tribesmen were eager to trade gold and diamonds for simple things like salt, sugar and mirrors. Being devout Muslims, they soon pressed their Islamic religion on the Bangu-Bangu people.

Some of the Arabs took Congolese women and had children with them. This strengthened their position and influence in the community. The Arabic fathers were accepted more fully and given positions of influence within the hierarchy of power. "After all," the Bangu-Bangus said, "these men are part of our family now. They would never do us any harm."

Unfortunately, they were wrong. Those same Arabic brothers-in-law saw the exceptional height and physical strength of the Bangu-Bangu men and realized that these Africans were exactly the kind that traded well in the slave markets of the world. They began a ruthless campaign of seizing the tribesmen and trading them to the Europeans as slaves.

It took several generations following the devastating slave era for the Bangu-Bangu tribe to re-establish, but throughout the process, the Lwamba family was able to maintain control of Kabambare kingdom which stretched from modern day Kivu to as far south as Shaba (Katanga) province.

The Lwamba monarchical family lived in the village of Kabambare, situated in the most southerly part of Kivu near the border of Burundi. Not all the people in the heavily populated area were Lwambas. There were other Bantu families conquered along the way in tribal conflicts. According to custom, conquered peoples became servants and workers for the victorious royal family and were required to give as tribute to the king a share of whatever they earned. In the vicinity of Kabambare, tribute most often took the form of gold and diamonds which, over time, added up to a sizable fortune for the Lwamba patriarch.

In keeping with tribal culture and Islamic tradition, it was common for the king to strengthen both his honour and his power base by taking multiple wives.

The more sons a man had, the more powerful his tribe would be and the greater the likelihood of victory in a conflict. Since it was also customary for heirs to the royal line to have at least four wives, it is not surprising the clan grew to significant proportions.

The tribal way of life came into jeopardy with the advent of Belgian colonization, following Henry Morton Stanley's exploration of the Congo Basin in the mid-1870s. Stanley, a British adventurer and journalist, carried back glowing reports to Europe about the Congo territory and its lavish trove of natural treasures.

King Leopold of Belgium was attracted to the bountiful rubber resources. He immediately set about acquiring a district for himself in Congo that was 10 times the size of his entire kingdom of Belgium.

Leopold and others like him made immense fortunes in Congo by ruthless exploitation of the native Congolese. Such brutal methods of forced labour were implemented during Leopold's rule there (1885 to 1908) that the population of Congo declined by half, from 20 million to 10 million people.

If labourers did not meet the stipulated quota of rubber, ivory or cotton, as set by the Belgian state, the penalty was flogging, mutilation or death. Flogging was inflicted with a chicotte, a whip made from strips of dried hippopotamus hide that could lay open the skin if applied sparingly or kill if used with enthusiasm. Bosses of labour gangs frequently brought in baskets filled with severed human hands to prove to their superiors they were doing their job. Because of Congo's hot and humid climate, the hands were sometimes smoked to preserve them.

News of such atrocities eventually leaked out to the rest of the world and Leopold was pressured into turning over his Congo possessions to the Belgian government in 1908. What had been a collection of privately owned properties became an official Belgian colony.

The relationship between the Belgian masters and Alondo-Modilo-Amalenge Lwamba, the king of Kabambare at the time, was strictly trade based. The Africans were eager to acquire salt and sugar, commodities that were always in short supply; the Belgians were more than happy to trade for gold, something the tribespeople had in abundance.

But beyond the parameters of Kabambare village, the European colonists were holding a hard line on the African population. The country, now known as the Belgian Congo or Congo Belgique, was governed with a rigid paternalism that was characteristic of the Belgian style of rule. Control was absolute. Any resistance to Belgian authority invited severe punishment, even death.

While it is true that the Belgians were establishing schools, developing industry, even offering technical training to a few select native Africans, the Congolese were only allowed to progress so far. No Black man could hold a top business position or political office.

The Belgians also brought Christianity to the Congo. In urban areas, Roman Catholicism was enforced comprehensively and absolutely. Interestingly, in the areas like Kasongo and Kabambare, where the Arabic/Islamic influence was long entrenched, the Belgians did not press the issue and by and large left the fierce warrior Bantus alone.

Though the Belgian colonist government professed to be coming in peace (unlike the regime under King Leopold), it appeared that the foreigners were using Christianity as a weapon to gain control of the country and its rich resources. Religious affiliation with the Catholic Church was a requirement for nearly every aspect of life. The Africans were forced to convert and be baptized in the Church; without baptism papers, one could not gain employment or pursue any form of education.

The requirement of a French name was another practice initiated by law in the earliest days of Belgian colonization. Without a French name, an African was considered indecent, untrustworthy and subhuman. Every African baby born was named not by the parents, but by their Belgian master.

It was into this milieu that Gilbert Ramadhani Biosubula Lwamba, the heir-apparent to the Lwamba royal line and the father of Michel, Fabian and Aliston, was born in 1929.

Until then, few Congolese had been educated, but that was about to change. The Belgians were intent on establishing a program to educate the brightest young African boys. They wanted to teach the young natives leadership skills and French so they could be liaisons between the Belgians and Congolese.

As a bright young man and the eldest son of a powerful tribal king, Gilbert was an obvious candidate for education. First, however, the Belgians had to convince Gilbert's father, the six-foot-seven giant, King Alondo-Modilo-Amalenge Lwamba, that no harm would come to the royal heir and that once educated, Gilbert would be a better king.

It was not an easy sell. Tribal culture believed that anyone who went to school was lazy. The majority of villagers couldn't understand why someone would want to spend his time reading and writing when he could be out hunting or digging for gold.

But Alondo-Modilo gave his permission and Gilbert was taken from Kabambare to Kasongo where he was put into a Belgian-run Roman Catholic mission school. Gilbert complied with the system's requirement that he become a member of the Roman Catholic Church, but his compliance caused ongoing strife between Gilbert and his Muslim-rooted family that lasted for many years.

At Belgian parochial schools, Congolese students were taught the skills of leadership and given opportunities to learn responsibility. They were encouraged to look analytically at how the government functioned and consider ways it could be improved. Gilbert Lwamba was fascinated by the process of government. He loved the whole political arena and the more he learned about it, the more he yearned to be a part of it.

The tribal royal heir did well in school and was very popular. His intelligence and friendly personality drew people like a magnet and his circle of friends included the brightest and best of both Black and White cultures in Congo. Even the priests took a special interest in the tall, good-looking young man who towered head and shoulders above most of them.

Gilbert's first job after high school was working for the government on an airport construction project in nearby Burundi. At the time, Burundi and Rwanda were known as Belgian Trusts and considered part of Congo. Lwamba, who learned to speak French fluently, was placed in charge of hiring African workers for the project. He spent a good deal of time at the airport construction site and became very familiar with the personnel there, including many of the airline pilots. Later on, he would invest a large amount of money in the national airline and buy up a chunk of farmland adjacent to the airport. On this, he established a profitable rice plantation and the Lwamba family spent many happy summers there.

At the age of 30, Gilbert enrolled in political studies at the University of Lubumbashi. In so doing, he was one of a very exclusive circle. Prior to 1960, when the Belgians were forced to hand over control of the country to the Africans, only 17 Congolese had received university degrees. Perhaps one explanation for this is that under the Belgian system, no Congolese could attend university until they had worked for the system for at least three to five years. During that time, half the candidate's wage was kept back and set aside to cover the university tuition. However, when the person actually completed his university training, he was required to pay back the money the government had "loaned" him for the tuition. It was a ludicrous arrangement, but the rule, nevertheless.

Nor was the educational system like that of any Western country. To complete a year of study, all classes had to be successfully passed. One failure meant repeating the entire year—and every subject—all over again. An added incentive to do well was the promise of a public beating at the hands of the Belgian authorities if the student failed.

Beatings and public punishment were an everyday occurrence in Congo. Each morning commenced with punishment—not just for students or errant children, but also for adults. To resist meant even harsher consequences. A child who missed a day of school and could not produce a satisfactory explanation for the absence was forced to witness his parents being humiliated before the whole town and slapped repeatedly across the face.

There were rules for everything in those days. Most made no sense at all.

Communities were strictly divided into Belgian and Congolese areas and any Congolese who ventured into a Belgian area was severely punished. A tradesman coming with live poultry to sell to the Europeans dared not let his chicken squawk. If it did, the offending bird was banged against the tradesman's head until it died.

Perhaps it is no wonder that fierce resentment boiled just beneath the deceptively meek surface of the Congolese. More and more, thinking people were calling for reform and independence.

"If we are to continue living here," people told one another in their private conversations, "things have got to change."

One Congolese who publicly and fervently spoke out about independence was Patrice Emergy Lumumba, a fiery young man from Kindu, not far from Gilbert Lwamba's hometown of Kabambare. Lumumba was on the lookout for bright, progressive men who might be persuaded to align themselves with his ideologies and join his Mouvement National Congolais (MNC) party.

Gilbert, by this time, had been promoted by the Belgian government to a position within the Ministry of Trade and Finance and as such, he was part of a group of French-speaking Congolese who met frequently to discuss various topics—most often, politics. At one of those meetings, Gilbert met a Catholic priest who knew Patrice Lumumba and wanted Gilbert to meet the up-and-coming politician.

A meeting was arranged.

Lumumba had heard about Gilbert Lwamba and was eager to make his acquaintance.

For his part, Gilbert found Lumumba to be an engaging man with a quick sense of humour. Though Lumumba was deadly serious about his ideology and the cause of independence for Congo, he loved telling jokes and was an entertaining person to be around. Gilbert was also fascinated with what Lumumba had to say politically and though he never became a close personal friend, he embraced Lumumba's ideology and preached it throughout the area of Lubumbashi where he now lived.

The latent but widespread hostility among Congolese toward Belgian rule brought Patrice Lumumba and his Mouvement National Congolais to the forefront in the late 1950s. The break with Belgium began peacefully enough. It started as a round table discussion, but things got out of hand in early 1959 when nationalist riots rocked the capital of Kinshasa. The Belgians quickly decided their vast economic interests in the country would be best protected by allowing immediate independence and free elections.

On June 30, 1960, Patrice Emergy Lumumba became the first premier of the newly liberated Republic of Congo.

His hold on the reins of government was tenuous. Leadership disputes, tribal dissension, abysmal literacy rates, a serious lack of trained Congolese leaders and a state of virtual economic and governmental shutdown, thanks to the exodus of Belgians who were leaving the country in droves, fearing for their lives, left the country in a state of chaos. Lumumba was forced to rely on the Belgian army to maintain order, but that didn't last long after some of the soldiers in the Force Publique (the Belgian Congolese Army) mutinied against their Belgian officers.

To add to the trouble, Congo's rich mining province of Katanga, which provided two-thirds of the country's revenue, decided to break away. The Soviet Union became involved, threatening unilateral intervention under the guise of supporting the Congolese against the Belgian oppressors. That set American nerves on edge and prompted a memo from the highest American government levels to eliminate Lumumba.

He, in the meantime, had appealed to the United Nations for aid in reorganizing the Congolese national army, and within weeks there were more than 16,000 UN troops in the Republic of Congo.

After months of confusion and violence, some semblance of order was restored, but it was too late for Patrice Emergy Lumumba. He was brutally tortured and murdered and the Belgian Congo became the Republic of Zaire under the rule of President Joseph Kasavubu. In the wings, General Joseph Désiré Mobutu, a journalist who had functioned as Patrice Lumumba's personal aide and then his army chief of staff, was elbowing his way into position to overthrow Kasavubu and seize control of the newly formed Zaire for himself.

Chapter Two

Joseph Désiré Mobutu was something of an unknown in Congolese circles. He came from the Ngbandi ethnic group, one of the smaller of Congo's 200 or so tribal groupings. The Ngbandis trace themselves back to the Nilotes peoples, originally an agrarian culture in central Sudan. To escape slave raids and Islamization, the Nilotiques—as they were known—moved south, first to Rwanda and Burundi where the Hutu and Tutsi tribes were already living, and eventually into north-eastern Zaire in search of fertile pasture land for their cattle.

The Nilotiques were foreigners to the Bantus in the area. Even their language was strange. They settled in the northern region, now known as Equateur province, and though generally perceived as backward and unrefined, they had a reputation for being good hunters.

Mobutu was born in Lisala, Belgian Congo. His father, a cook, died when he was young and Mobutu was raised by his mother, who worked as a hotel maid. His earliest education was in Léopoldville, but later his mother sent him to the Christian Brothers boarding school in Coquilhatville. In 1949, he joined the Force Publique, the Belgian Congolese army, where he rose to the rank of sergeant.

In 1956, Mobutu left the army and became a journalist for *L'Avenir*, Léopoldville's daily paper. It was through his journalistic endeavours that he became acquainted with Patrice Lumumba and the Mouvement National Congolais (MNC) party.

During his reign as president, Mobutu's home village of Gbadolite became an entity unto itself. He built an outrageously extravagant palace that journalists nicknamed "Versailles in the Jungle." Gbadolite was also the headquarters and training grounds for the dreaded DSP (Special Presidential Division), Mobutu's elite security unit dedicated to his own personal protection. Unit members were recruited almost entirely from the Ngbandi tribe and trained by Israelis in the deadly skill of murder and torture.

Everywhere else in Zaire one could travel freely, but to enter Gbadolite required a passport. Where commodity prices across the rest of Zaire were uniformly sky-high, in Mobutu's village they were at rock bottom, despite the fact that the economy there was reported to be higher than almost any other place in the world. Five dollars bought next to nothing elsewhere, yet secured rent in Gbadolite. It was a strictly closed community and people on the outside understood that strangers venturing into Gbadolite were putting their lives in jeopardy.

At the beginning of Mobutu's presidency, the Congolese people supported him enthusiastically, believing his desire for democratic change matched Patrice Lumumba's and their own. But they soon realized Mobutu had a very different agenda.

Lumumba's MNC party was banished and replaced with Mobutu's Mouvement Populaire de la Révolution (People's Revolution Movement) or MPR. It became the nation's only legal political party and the one every citizen was required to join. Later on, Mobutu would hold presidential elections where he would win 99% of the popular vote because voting was compulsory and Mobutu was the only candidate.

The dictatorial edicts and bizarre legislation that began to flow made discerning citizens quickly realize that the regime of Joseph Désiré Mobutu made all that had gone on before look tame.

Opposition to Mobutu was dealt with furiously and forcibly. In 1966, four cabinet ministers were arrested on charges of complicity in an attempted coup. They were publicly executed in an open-air spectacle attended by over 50,000 people as an example of what would happen to anyone who opposed the president.

Through this transition period, Gilbert Lwamba continued in his government position, though he was badly shaken by Lumumba's death and demise of the MNC dream. He did not believe that Joseph Mobutu would bring the peace and democratic government to Zaire that people desired. Time would show his reservations were well founded.

In terms of position and economics, Gilbert prospered under the Mobutu government. Because of his education and administrative experience, he was appointed advisor to the governor of Shaba province.

Quite apart from the familial assets that were his by right as the royal heir, he was also amassing considerable wealth on his own. Gilbert already owned several houses and large land tracts in various parts of Zaire and Burundi. A portion of the rice plantation adjacent to Burundi's airport was purchased for a handsome sum when the city of Bujumbura needed it for expansion purposes.

The country houses were used mostly for summering and vacations, but Gilbert had other motives for keeping them, especially the farm in Burundi. He wanted to have a safe place where his family could go and hide in case things got out of hand in Zaire. Little did he know the day would come soon enough when neither Burundi nor anywhere else in central Africa would be a safe haven for his family.

The Lwambas' main residence was in Lubumbashi, a city of about three million. Unlike some of his fellow countrymen, Gilbert was not content to live in one of the elaborate residences left behind by the Belgians. He moved his family to Belaire, an affluent residential neighbourhood in Lubumbashi, where he had a palatial home custom built. It was beautiful inside and out. The sprawling building with multiple wings was finished with an elegant vanilla-coloured exterior and surrounded by towering trees and lush gardens. The property was enclosed in a high wall that extended about ten metres in front of the house. The walled compound was constantly guarded by armed security personnel who were supplied to all government officials or influential business people in Zaire.

While Gilbert enjoyed the fine things his wealth afforded, he also liked working with his hands. It was not uncommon for him to come home from his government office and launch into a building project or a repair job. On one occasion, people in the neighbourhood were dumbfounded to see the deputy governor out early one morning mowing his own grass in front of the mansion.

The Lubumbashi house was designed to accommodate a large family. In keeping with tribal and Muslim custom, Gilbert had two wives who lived in different wings of the spacious residence. His children thought of the two women in the typical African fashion: as their two mothers. Terms like "half-brother" or "your mother and my mother" did not exist. Everyone was family.

Besides the two women, the household consisted of a dozen immediate family members, plus extended relatives and servants. In African culture, it is not unusual for a sister and all her children to live in a brother's home, especially if the brother could easily support the extra members.

Gilbert Lwamba had four children with his first wife Jane: Cecile, who would eventually marry Zairean National Television journalist Mesombuko Saidi Zamarudi; George, who was born in 1965 and named after Gilbert's father; and two other girls, Leonie and Julienne.

Gilbert's second wife was Edwine Mwadjuma. They had five children together.

Michel Mbundanini was born in 1967 and named after Gilbert's oldest brother.

Fabian Selemani, the namesake of Gilbert's second brother, was born in 1972. The elder Fabian Selemani attended the same Belgian mission school as Gilbert and in adulthood, visited the Lwamba household often.

Aliston Ndalbandu, born in 1978, bears the Muslim name of Gilbert's youngest brother Ali.

Two girls were also born to Gilbert and Edwine: Elizabeth, in 1971, and Gisele, in 1983.

Like Gilbert, Edwine was well educated. She had a high school diploma and spent one year at university before her parents refused to spend any more money on her education. "Women," they said, "are meant to get married and produce children."

Edwine's children remember her as being a wonderful woman who invested deeply in the lives of her children. She was a loving mother and shared her time generously, looking after their every need. Most of all, they remember her fun-loving nature and the happy times they had with her.

One of their father's outstanding qualities was his sage wisdom. Though not a particularly religious man, Gilbert had strong values and principles. He liked to use parables and object lessons to teach life principles.

Aliston remembers one object lesson through which Gilbert taught the boys to be loving and share whatever they had.

"He showed us how to share a nut by dividing it up," Aliston recalls. "He said the nut could be for one person or for all of us. Our father wanted us to understand that we shouldn't have any divisions between us. Any time I ate a nut after that without sharing it, I felt I had committed a great sin."

Both Gilbert and Edwine did their best to instill high ideals in their children. Seeing what was going on around them, Gilbert wanted to prepare his sons for the future. The most important lesson he taught the boys was to keep the family united, no matter what. It was a lesson that would serve them well in the years to come.

"Our father said we needed to be united in everything," Fabian remembers. "He liked to see all of us together for lunch and for supper. He wouldn't start eating if one of us was missing and he would phone if he couldn't be home himself. That doesn't happen in many families in Africa. Sometimes a man will have five or six wives. They're all living together, but the father doesn't even know the names of his children, nor how many he has. Our father was very passionate about us. He was always there, setting a good example."

One day Gilbert gathered his four sons around him. He picked up four thin sticks and put them together in a little bundle. He handed the bundle to George.

"Can you break these?" he asked.

George tried and couldn't.

Gilbert gave the bundle to Michel and asked the same question. "Can you break these?"

Michel couldn't. Neither could Fabian nor Aliston.

Gilbert took the sticks in his hand. "You can't break these sticks because you are not strong enough," he said. "But I can break them."

One by one, he removed the sticks from the bundle and broke them.

"In your life," he told his four sons, "if you do not stick together, you will be broken—just like these sticks. But if you stay united, not one of you will be broken."

In their darkest hours, his boys would remember those words and cling to their father's wisdom.

Gilbert Lwamba was also concerned about the people outside of his family. His concern for his sons' friends was no secret. "You were born into a wealthy family and have everything you need," he often told his boys, "but remember, you have to share—not just with your family, but with everyone else who is in need."

Gilbert was a firm believer in human rights and treating people with dignity and respect. It was a concept unheard of in the Congo under Belgian colonial rule and was an equally alien ideology under the emerging leadership of Joseph Mobutu. The president was enacting change, all right, but none of it addressed human rights.

The changes began the moment Mobutu took office in November of 1960. His first act was to replace the old Congolese flag with a new one showing a black fist clenching a flaming torch. Geographical place names were the next things to go. The capital, Léopoldville, became Kinshasa; Elizabethville, where the Lwambas lived, was renamed Lubumbashi.

The public and MNC party proponents, in particular, questioned the move. "This was not the kind of change we have been calling for," they said. "Why are you changing the country's name? We want you to change more important things—like the government's behaviour and the socio-economic state of people's lives."

The name changes were just the beginning. Mobutu decreed that all French names must be abandoned and African names revived and used exclusively. Priests were warned they would face five years' imprisonment if they baptized a Zairean child with a Christian name. Mobutu set the tone by renaming himself Mobutu Sese Seko Kuku Ngbendu Wa Za Banga or The All-Powerful Warrior Who Because of His Endurance and Inflexible Will to Win, Will Go From Conquest to Conquest Leaving Fire in His Wake.

Not everyone in the new Zaire was eager to give up their European name. Nor were people inclined to obey the edict from the top that said every document or certificate bearing the person's French name must be destroyed. Suddenly it was illegal to own anything that smacked of the Belgian era, including the old Congolese flag. Wearing Western business suits and ties like the Belgians was also unlawful.

"We have our own African dress that everyone must wear," Mobutu said, referring to the high-collared jacket that was his own fashion invention. Known as the *abacost* (from "à bas le costume" or "down with the jacket"), it came in dark brown or navy blue wool—both of which were grossly unsuited to the country's tropical climate.

Gilbert Lwamba refused to make the switch. "You cannot abolish everything the Belgians brought," he told his superior. "There are many good things like schools, buildings and education. If it weren't for the Belgians, I would not know how to read or write."

He also refused to burn the photos and documents that pertained to his life under colonial rule. "These things are part of who I am," he declared. "The pictures were taken when I was a young boy in school. We cannot erase everything from our memory. Yes, we need to do away with the bad things, but wearing a necktie and a business suit doesn't make me less of a man—less Zairean. Let us focus on more important things."

Gilbert continued to wear his European-style suits and neckties. Sometimes it meant arrest and being held in detention, but because of his high profile and his popularity with the people, he was never imprisoned. Others were not so lucky. Many caught wearing neckties were strung up by their own ties and hanged.

Soon there were more rules. Many seemed ad hoc, according to the president's whim on any given day. One law required the entire Zairean population to perform traditional African dances in praise of the president before starting work each day and for 25 minutes every Friday. At the specified times, employees of all businesses, directors of all corporations, headmasters, professors and students in educational institutions—indeed, all of Zaire—had to stop what they were doing and sing and dance in praise of President Mobutu Sese Seko.

Under Mobutu, corruption became the byword of the day. He encouraged it and went as far as passing Article 15, legislation that effectively said to Zaireans: "If you need it, it's your right to take it." "If you want to steal, steal a little in a nice way," he told the people of Zaire. "But if you steal too much to become rich overnight, you'll be caught."

Mobutu was the worst offender of all those who abused government funds. At one point, he held three positions simultaneously: president, prime minister and general of the army and collected salaries from all three posts. His growing personal wealth would eventually rank him as the fourth richest man in the world. It was said that Mobutu's personal fortune was big enough to have wiped out the country's national debt.

Mobutu's children were as corrupt as he was and considered themselves above the law. It was not uncommon for his 18-year-old and 22-year-old sons to go into a bar, kill whomever they chose for no apparent reason and receive no jail time or even a reprimand for the crime. National television reported that one of Mobutu's sons visited a Swiss bank to withdraw money from his father's account. When a bank employee informed him that banking hours were over, young Mobutu pulled a gun and shot the man dead. He was arrested, but Swiss authorities released him after his father paid a very large sum of money to the man's widow.

Many times, the younger Mobutus would enter a Zairean bank, point to the face on the currency and declare, "This is my father, so the money in this bank belongs to me and I am taking it."

Similarly, they would walk into private homes and announce, "I want this house." The owners had no recourse but to walk out immediately and leave everything behind.

The president's youngest son had a reputation for breaking up weddings, whisking away the bride and raping her before giving her back to her new husband.

The bullying and abuse of power got so out of hand that during a soccer game in which the team Mobutu's uncle favoured was losing, the uncle declared a change in the official rules of soccer that extended the game until his team won.

Rumours of atrocities at the hands of Mobutu and his thugs were rampant. People were outraged and aghast, but few dared to speak out. Many who did disappeared.

Gilbert Lwamba was one who refused to keep silent. He was disgusted by the things being done to Zairean citizens by their own president and his government that were clearly against the United Nation's view of human rights. He refused to put his signature to the many papers and directives that would mean ultimate harm for his fellow Congolese. He knew full well that he was putting his own life on the line, but he believed his background, his high profile and public sentiment would keep him safe. More and more, though, Gilbert could foresee the day when Zaire would no longer be a safe place for his family.

He began talking about leaving his job, leaving Zaire, finding a place in another African country where they could all live safely and he could pursue his farming interests. He said to his four sons, "If anything happens to me, make sure you stay focused and united."

"What is happening in our country is not right," Gilbert would muse aloud to them. "I am getting paid, but the parents of your friends are not. You live comfortably under this roof, but your friends outside are suffering. They come here, I give them food, they see the way we live, they want to live the same way and they have the right to do that. Their fathers are working hard and deserve a good salary, but they're not getting one. It isn't right at all."

On one occasion when Lwamba mentioned his concerns to the president, Mobutu shot back, "What is this? Are you working behind my back to overthrow me? I know your background, Lwamba. Could it be you want to be president? Are you just waiting for me to step down from this chair so you can occupy it?"

Other things were raising Mobutu's suspicions about Gilbert's motives. He knew that Lwamba met with his old friends from the MNC party on a regular basis.

It greatly alarmed Mobutu, who was kept informed about the meetings. Why, he wanted to know, were these men gathering together like that? Was someone calling them together? Could it be they had designs on his presidency? He had already protected himself by legislating a political system where, to be a candidate for election, one had to be the founder of his MPR party (Movement Populaire de la Révolution or the People's Revolution Movement). And since he was the sole founder, only he could stand for election. So what was going on? Were these people planning a coup?

When Mobutu discovered that Gilbert Lwamba was responsible for bringing the old group together, he demanded the gatherings stop. This demand seemed unreasonable to Gilbert. He was increasingly frustrated with the shocking corruption of Mobutu's regime and considered resigning, but he knew it was a dangerous thing to do. Anyone who resigned from Mobutu's government generally ended up dead, or kidnapped and tortured, or brainwashed so he could not reveal all the secret things in which he knew the government was involved. Most government officials who wanted to resign went abroad and sent back their resignations by mail.

A former education minister under Patrice Lumumba was lured back to Zaire from exile under the belief that Mobutu was offering him amnesty. Instead, he was tortured and killed. While still alive, his eyes were gouged out, his genitals ripped off and his limbs amputated one by one. The gruesome murder was an object lesson to any others who might be considering leaving Mobutu's government and exposing its repression and corruption to the world.

Despite knowing that a resignation from government was a self-imposed death sentence, Gilbert Lwamba refused to be intimidated. He would eventually resign in 1987. From that moment on, his family would be under careful scrutiny from Mobutu's special agents.

Chapter Three

MOST OF THE LWAMBA CHILDREN ATTENDED SECONDARY SCHOOL AT BUKAVU where there was a good Catholic school run by the French and Belgians. Since Gilbert was well known and respected in the area, he believed it would be safe for his children to be educated there.

Gilbert wanted the best in education for his children. To his mind, education was all-important. In fact, it was so important that when Michel developed a fascination with the guitar at the age of six, Gilbert did his best to discourage his son. He had visions of Michel growing up to be a shiftless rock musician, rather than following the lofty family tradition of politics and a position in government.

Despite Gilbert's misgivings, he was unable to entirely disassociate his children from music. Nor did he intend to. Music is an integral part of African life. No party or family gathering was complete without everyone participating in a time of spontaneous singing and dancing. For Africans, singing is a means of relaxation and refreshment for the mind and soul. In the villages, people use every opportunity possible to come together and celebrate by dancing and singing the traditional tribal songs.

The Lwamba home in Lubumbashi always seemed to be abuzz with visitors. Many came from the familial village of Kabambare in Kivu province. Though the urban mansion was furnished with all the modern amenities, the gathering inevitably moved outdoors around a bonfire. Before long, everyone was singing to the music of a drummer and moving around the fire in traditional dances.

The Lwamba children grew up with this spontaneous sort of music and began participating early. As youngsters, they learned all the traditional village songs and dances and if they didn't understand all the Bangu-Bangu words, the visitors from Kabambare were happy to translate.

While Michel loved those times of traditional dancing and singing, he was even more fascinated by the modern musical groups he saw on television. All the hottest acts from North America came to the Lwamba home daily via cable and satellite TV. Michel absorbed it like a sponge.

Early on, he fell in love with guitars.

"Would you please buy me one?" he asked his father.

"No," Gilbert replied calmly. "I want you to go to school, not become a musician." The look of disappointment on Michel's face made him add, "I'll buy you a guitar when you finish university."

To a seven-year-old, finishing university was light years away. Michel knew he couldn't wait that long. Watching his heroes, the great North American musicians, on television made him more impatient with each passing day. He didn't know the stars' names and couldn't understand a word of their English lyrics. He just knew he loved the sound and the style of their music.

And so, at the tender age of seven, Michel awoke one morning and said to himself, "I'm going to make myself a guitar."

His eyes fell upon a wooden toy his father had recently made for his birthday. It was a push toy—a wooden-wheeled car that was propelled by a long stick. Gilbert had spent hours in his workshop fashioning the toy.

But Michel could see another potential in the car. He took it apart, discarded the wheels and attached the long stick to a jerry can. He fastened a length of nylon string to the two pieces and used the tops of ballpoint pens for pegs, making holes in them through which to thread the string.

He was playing with his guitar when his father came home from work.

The first thing Gilbert noticed was the discarded wheels.

"What happened to your car?" he asked his son.

Michel hesitated. "I took it apart to make a guitar."

His father fixed him with a stern eye. "Why did you do that? I spent a lot of time making that toy for you. If you didn't like it, you should have said so instead of breaking it apart."

Michel was grounded for a week for destroying his birthday gift, but to his relief, his father did not confiscate the guitar.

"It was part of my father's belief to respect a person's rights," he says, "even if that person was a young child."

So every evening for a week young Michel was banished to his room after supper. But he had his guitar for company. He practised and practised on the fretless guitar, trying to reproduce the sounds he knew a guitar should make. Even after the grounding was over, he would go to his room every day after school to play.

It was about that time that Michel had the opportunity to hold a real guitar for the first time. It was too big for him, of course, but the experience was unforgettable.

As time went on, Michel and Fabian began going to a Christian church with friends. The attraction was not the preaching or the message. It was the music— the choir, the songs and the instrumentalists. Michel loved watching the guitarists make music with their instruments. His eyes followed every movement. Afterward, he would go home and try to replicate it on his homemade guitar. It wasn't easy. For one thing, he didn't know how to tune his instrument and he played on only one string. Nevertheless, he became amazingly skilled at reproducing the tunes.

He also began composing his own melodies. He wrote them down, though they didn't make any sense because he didn't know the first thing about reading or writing music. His compositions were a fusion of the music he saw on television, the songs he heard in church and the music the village people sang.

The more Michel's ability and fascination with music grew, the more alarmed his father became. Gilbert was convinced his second son would never finish school. But he needn't have worried. Music gave Michel the incentive to do well at school so he could go home quickly and teach himself something new on his guitar.

Eventually he approached a guitar teacher about taking lessons.

"What can you play?" the man asked. "Do you know any songs?"

"Yes," Michel replied confidently and proceeded to play a one-string tune on his homemade guitar.

The teacher laughed. "I'll teach you the notes and how to read music," he said, "but I'm much too busy to do more than that."

It was a start.

Once he had learned the basics, Michel absorbed whatever else he could from textbooks and other guitarists. Mostly he learned from hours and hours of practising and experimenting.

After five years of this, he went back to his father. "I really need a guitar," he said bluntly.

By this time, Gilbert was well aware of his young son's ability and he must surely have been proud of Michel's determination and patience.

"You have persevered a long time," he said, "and you've been content to play that homemade guitar. You're right. It is time you had a real guitar."

Soon afterward, Michel got his first real guitar and the homemade one was passed on to Fabian.

Three years younger, Fabian shared Michel's passion for music and was fast becoming a ready partner in his brother's musical endeavours. He was eager to learn everything Michel could teach him.

The two began singing together. When they perceived their vocal sound needed a third voice, they coerced their younger brother Aliston to sing with them.

Aliston resisted and sometimes it took some force to make him compliant.

"Aliston doesn't have to sing if he doesn't want to," Gilbert would scold the other two boys. "You can't force him."

But as soon as their father was out of sight, Michel and Fabian would pull Aliston over and make him sing again. It wasn't an ideal learning arrangement, since the two older boys were not above yelling at their younger brother when his vocalizing didn't quite meet their expectations. Eventually, Aliston developed a keen musical ear and a smooth vocal style that people remarked on with pleasure.

Together, the three Lwamba brothers amassed a broad repertoire of vocal and instrumental music. Some of it was music they heard on television or in church; some of it was music of the village. They continued to be inspired by the music they saw on cable television and often blended those genres with traditional village music just to make it more interesting.

Before long, the three were being invited to sing publicly. Their very first performance was in church. The congregation loved them. Other invitations came. The boys even went so far as to make some tapes of their singing in a little recording studio in the church.

They had no illusions about their musicianship. The singing was simply for fun, as was the instrumental music. Still, as they watched television performers like Michael Jackson being wildly acclaimed and applauded, they couldn't help thinking how thrilling it would be to have people applaud like that for them.

The only Canadian musician the three knew was Bryan Adams. Michel, especially, was fascinated by Adams' unique singing style. He had no idea what the performer was singing because all the words were in English. He and his brothers tried to imitate the lyrics, often throwing in French words that sounded similar to the English ones.

Copying someone else's music quickly lost its appeal for the brothers, who were discovering they had a genuine talent for writing music and lyrics of their own. What's more, people loved the pieces they performed.

By the time Michel and Fabian entered university, they were accomplished musicians and part of a band that played at all the significant campus and community events. The music was a pleasant diversion from the demands of university life and the disturbing things that were going on all around them.

Michel and Fabian had enrolled in their father's alma mater, the University of Lubumbashi, the second largest university in Zaire and at one time, the largest in all of Africa. Established by the Belgians, the University of Lubumbashi had an excellent reputation and was the learning institution of choice in the country. Many of the professors had studied abroad and were considered authorities in their fields.

Michel entered the University of Lubumbashi in 1987. Following the example of his father, he enrolled in political science. Fabian enrolled the next year, also in political science.

As was the custom, they lived in the university dormitories. Living on the campus made it easier to study and work on assignments. On weekends, they went home to their family.

Those college years should have been the best time of their lives, but Zaire's difficulties and growing instability were sharply mirrored on the campus. Living conditions had changed little since the '50s, when Gilbert Lwamba attended. Students were still responsible for cooking their own meals. The Lwamba brothers were privileged in that they had a small garden plot outside the dorm and a portable stove. Others were not so lucky. Most were too poor to afford even a small cooker. One student spent three years cooking his meals on an overturned electric iron.

Outside the university, jobs were quickly disappearing. Infrastructure in Zaire had deteriorated almost completely. Roads were crumbling. There was no telephone service. The currency had little value. The economy had shrunk and so had the salaries of those still lucky enough to be receiving one.

The economic inequity was monstrous. Despite the fact that Zaire's immense gold, diamond and mineral resources made it the richest country in Africa, Mobutu was putting an ever larger chunk of the national revenues in his already bulging pocket. As a result, Zaire had become one of the poorest coun-tries in the world.

Many Zairean workers received no salary at all. For teachers in government-run schools, wages were nonexistent, even though they had worked for the system most of their lives. Their only income was the bribe money paid by par-ents to ensure their children got good grades.

There were private religious schools, of course, like the ones the Lwamba children attended. There, teachers' wages came out of tuition fees. But only a small percentage of the population could afford to send their children to such schools.

The professors and instructors at the University of Lubumbashi had gone for an alarmingly long time without wages. At the best of times, a full professor earned only about $300 a month, despite the fact he could have gone—at great personal expense and sacrifice—to study at a prestigious North American uni-versity. It was passion for their discipline and hope for their country's future that pulled them back to their lecture halls each day.

No one was more acutely aware of how badly Zaire was deteriorating than the students in the political science department.

"We used to hear on the radio and on television about democracy and how things were changing for the better in other parts of the world," Fabian recalls. "It seemed to us we were the only country on earth that didn't have a democ-ratic government. And we wanted democracy. We desperately wanted freedom."

Professors who had studied in North America spoke eloquently about democracy, secure in the belief that because they were appointed to the teaching staff long before Mobutu came on the scene, their positions were secure. And perhaps they were. Being intelligent, well-qualified specialists, respected in their areas of discipline, they were exactly the kind of people the dictator-president needed around him to give him credibility in the global community. To that end, he had made several of them ministers in his government. But they had to be careful. Some professors told of their attempts to persuade Mobutu to abandon his agenda and his philosophies. When the president refused to listen to them, some resigned. Others mysteriously disappeared and were later reported dead.

Mysterious disappearances became more and more commonplace as the decade of the '80s advanced in Zaire. It seemed that anyone who raised a voice in protest or dissent wound up dead. Yet demands for democratic change continued.

At one point, it seemed the president might be taking the demands of his citizens to heart. In a speech at the University of Lubumbashi, he proclaimed, "Everything is going to change!"

When they heard that, the students were elated. They wanted so much to believe their president was speaking of change in positive political terms. Dared they speculate that the winds of democracy blowing around the world were finally shifting to Zaire? "Surely," they said, "these changes will be good for our country."

They were not.

Nor were the changes Mobutu articulated in another ambiguous statement a few months later. "Nothing," he said, "will ever be the same again."

At the university, there was a feeling of deep hopelessness. Students were working hard to complete their studies, but when they graduated, there were no jobs for them in the flattened Zairean economy. They saw their professors faithfully teaching classes month after month, getting no salary and not daring to demand the wages owed them.

Another issue was scholarships. According to the bylaws of the university, every student was entitled to a certain amount of money as an allowance from the government. What they were receiving was only a fraction of their entitlement.

"You would sign for $500, but receive only $100," Michel remembers. "Your other $400 was going into someone else's pockets. If you said, 'I'm not going to sign this,' they would reply, 'Then you don't get anything.' Some students spent five years receiving no allowance, even though it was recorded that they were being paid the full amount. Their money was going into the pockets of Mobutu's people."

The only way the students knew to express their outrage and vent their frustration over all these issues was to demonstrate. And indeed, public demonstration was a way of life for the students of the University of Lubumbashi.

The demonstrations were generally looked upon with tolerance by the local authorities, who were routinely dispatched to keep the peace. The authorities were soldiers in the regular army, the FAZ or Forces Armées Zaïroises. The soldiers were local people, many of them parents or friends of the students. The encounters were predictable. The troops would issue a warning; the students would throw a few stones. Shoes or other objects were tossed back; words were exchanged. Rarely was there any violence or injury. If a soldier was inadvertently hurt by a stone, the troops would shower the students with tear gas and the demonstration would come to an abrupt, but peaceable end.

The Lwamba brothers were deeply involved in a political movement, the Union for Democracy and Social Progress (UDSP), which had a strong following within and without the university. The student members met regularly to discuss the need for democratic change in Zaire. Michel was the president of the student movement; Fabian was in charge of soliciting membership.

The Zairean president was well aware of the student agitation and the growing strength of their political movement. At one point, he made a special trip from the capital of Kinshasa to Lubumbashi to address the university's 15,000 students.

Mobutu, who liked to involve his audiences in a friendly question/answer type of exchange, appeared to invite a response from the students when he asked, "What do you think should be done to help our country move forward?"

One student in the crowd dared to respond. Standing, he said, "I know someone who has been here for 10 years and is unable to do his work successfully. What should we do with him?"

"He should be thrown out," Mobutu replied. "It is clear this person is not capable of getting a higher education. He should find something else to do with his life."

"That student is you, Mr. Mobutu," the student shot back. "You have been the president in this country for 32 years and there have been no changes. You are doing nothing for our country, only looking out for your own interests. You should step down and let someone else take over."

It was a brave gesture, but a fatal one. A few days later, the student was found dead.

Following the incident at the university, the president initiated a surveillance program that placed soldiers on the campus 24 hours a day.

The soldiers were an overt symbol of Mobutu's authority and control. Behind the scenes, more sinister things were afoot.

The students continued to hold their UDSP meetings and plan their protest strategies. Their discussions covered many areas of concern and frustration like the president's actions, his role in the disappearance or death of certain individuals and the escalating problems at their university. They also talked about the feasibility of approaching the governor of the province to see if he could do something to improve conditions at the university. And, as always, they laid their plans for going into the streets of Lubumbashi to demonstrate for justice and change.

Since the president's disastrous address, however, every time the students mobilized and prepared to head for the streets, soldiers showed up to prevent the march. These were not the usual FAZ personnel. They were members of the DSP, the president's special security force, Ngbandis who answered directly to Mobutu.

Suspicions of an informer in their midst circulated among the students. It escalated when they began seeing reports of their UDSP meetings and their private discussions in the public newspaper.

There was something else. Although most students struggled to make do on their meagre allowances, the rooms of a few students were full of expensive gadgets—stereos, CD players and big screen televisions and they drove BMWs. The irony was that these seemingly affluent individuals were not particularly intelligent. They were, however, all Ngbandis from Mobutu's tribe and claimed to have scholarships from the president himself.

Suddenly, students began disappearing.

"We would notice that So-and-So wasn't there," Michel recalls. "We'd ask, 'Where is this person?' Sometimes the parents would come to the university asking about their son. 'Where is he?' they wanted to know. 'Why hasn't he come home?'"

In the next 8 weeks, 15 students disappeared. The one thing they had in common was that they had all spoken out at student UDSP meetings. Why, everyone wondered, were they disappearing and who would be next?

As leaders of the student movement, Michel and Fabian knew they were under scrutiny, but they felt a measure of security because of their royal background and their father's high profile.

Another element of security was living in a dormitory room with six other people. Most of the people who disappeared lived alone.

"We were like children in an orphanage," Fabian says. "Our beds were bunk beds and there were eight of us to a room. An arrangement like that made it difficult for anyone to enter the room and kidnap or kill just one person."

Who was responsible? That was the question on everyone's mind. Was it the Zairean military doing the killing? Not likely. There was no way military personnel from the outside could come into the buildings without the students knowing. It had to be an inside job.

Things came to a head one evening in the final days of April, 1989, after the students' attempts to mount a protest march from the university to downtown Lubumbashi were foiled yet again. Special security people armed with unusually heavy artillery had appeared at the campus gates and held the students at gunpoint.

It was obvious someone had leaked the plan to hold the protest. But who? The students were determined to find out.

A small group decided to do some investigating and began searching the lockers of four students known to be at the university on special scholarships. They found the lockers secured with padlocks of a kind not seen before in Zaire. It took some ingenuity and a good deal of force to break them open.

What the searchers found shocked them. The lockers were crammed full of high-powered automatic weapons, deadly looking knives, two-way radios and infrared night-vision helmets.

The discovery sent icy chills down the young peoples' spines. Where, they asked one another, would college students get infrared equipment? And, more importantly, why would anyone want it? Was there any possible explanation why a student would keep weapons capable of holding 100 bullets at a time in his locker? And then there were the knives....

When the searchers reported their findings, fear and panic seized the student group. Their first instinct was to go after the owners of the lockers, but first they enlisted the help of some fellow students who had a reputation for being "tough guys."

An impromptu posse located and seized three of *les mouchards* or cowards, as the locker owners were being called. The fourth escaped by jumping out of a fourth storey window. He miraculously survived the jump and was whisked away by special security agents who just happened to appear on the scene.

The students took the three and forced them to stand trial before a jury made up of members of the university's law department. A democratic trial was organized. The three men were assigned a lawyer. Three judges presided. The three *mouchards*, who turned out to be agents of President Mobutu's DSP unit masquerading as university students, were found guilty and sentenced to death.

Fueled by the evidence brought to bear in the trial and the reminder of the cold-blooded murders of their colleagues, the students dragged the agents outside and began beating them. The men would most likely have been beaten to death had not military helicopters buzzed in to disperse the mob and snatch up the three agents.

Two died in hospital. The third survived.

Mobutu's vengeance was swift and predictable. The very next morning, more students were found dead in their rooms, which told the survivors that *les trois mouchards* were not the only traitors within the student body.

By now, the entire population of the University of Lubumbashi felt threatened. No one went to class. "We are not going back to class until we have seen the governor about this," the students declared. "He needs to know that students are being murdered here. Maybe he can do something to stop the killings."

It was decided that a peaceful march from the campus to the governor's office in the city would be the best way to get his attention.

Chapter Four

THE MARCH TO THE GOVERNOR'S OFFICE WAS PLANNED FOR VERY EARLY ON THE morning of Tuesday, May 9.

The students never got off the campus.

As they approached the entrance gates, they found the military already there, surrounding the university, refusing to let them leave.

"We want to speak to the governor," the students declared. "It is our right. You can't stop us."

But the soldiers could and they did. The students had no defence against the heavily armed military presence.

Once again the question circulated: How did they know?

In the midst of the milieu, a student was spotted talking covertly on a two-way radio. When he realized he was being observed, he quickly hid the device in his clothing and disappeared into the crowd. But the sighting confirmed what the students already suspected. There were more infiltrators on campus than *les trois mouchards*.

The students clumped together in tight knots to discuss the situation and its implications. Those brave enough to challenge the confinement were told, "You have to stay here because someone from Kinshasa is coming to talk to you about what happened the other day."

The campus felt like a prison. Throughout the day, the front gates remained closed. Only students who had been off-campus were allowed in. No one went out.

The front entrance gates were the only entry/exit point to the University of Lubumbashi. The sprawling campus was situated a kilometre or so out of the city and was flanked by the Prison de Casapar on one side and the FAZ army base on the other. The third side was bordered by dense forest which led to endless miles of inhospitable wilderness and eventually the Zambian border. The students were completely trapped.

Some of the young people returned to their rooms and tried to study for upcoming exams; most stayed outdoors talking quietly, trying to make sense of what was happening. A few, like Michel and Fabian, were keeping a wary eye on the military presence. All day long they noticed military vehicles cruising around the campus.

There was a good deal of speculation about what that military presence might mean and what was likely to happen next. The hope was that the soldiers were there simply to keep the gates closed and once the unnamed "someone" from Kinshasa made his appearance, everything would be back to normal.

When 6:00 rolled around and the regular army soldiers began to depart, it looked as if the students might be right. They heaved a collective sigh of relief. Nothing was going to happen after all.

Then, at 8:00 the lights went out.

It wasn't the first time the electricity had gone off at the University of Lubumbashi. Normally, the polytechnic students were summoned to fix the outage and restore power. Today, out of habit, they headed for the powerhouse.

When they reached the little building, they found it ringed by heavily armed security guards.

"What are you doing here?" the guards demanded.

"We've come to switch on the electricity so we can have some light," the students replied.

"Back off," one soldier snarled. "If you come any closer, we'll shoot you."

It was at this point that the students realized the men they were facing were not the regular FAZ soldiers they were accustomed to seeing. These were different people: cold, aggressive, speaking an unfamiliar dialect.

"Take two more steps and we'll kill you," another growled.

Bewildered and now thoroughly apprehensive, the students retreated into the blackness that engulfed the whole campus.

Then word came that the telephone lines were down.

Gradually, the horrible realization dawned. All contact with the outside world had been cut off. They were helpless prisoners on their own campus.

Four young people decided to take advantage of the darkness and make a break for the city, but as they neared the front gates, a powerful torch light pinned them in its beam.

"Don't go any further!" a soldier shouted. "We can see you! Go back!"

"How can they see us in the dark?" the students asked one another. "They're hundreds of feet away."

"We just want to go out and buy some candles," one of them called out. "You can't stop us. We're not prisoners."

"No one leaves. And no candles."

These students, too, were struck by the soldiers' unfamiliar accents. And they noticed something else: the number of armed personnel had swelled significantly.

The four made their way back to the crowd of clustered students. "We have to do something," they said. "This place is surrounded by soldiers."

Someone suggested lighting a bonfire. It seemed like a good idea, not only for the light it would provide, but for some badly needed heat to ward off the cold that was chilling them to the bone.

A fire was started and everyone went in search of wood to fuel it. Some collected kindling from the cafeteria; others scavenged dead branches from the towering trees that had shaded the campus buildings for years. Still others ventured into the nearby forest. They came back breathless, telling of armed soldiers moving through the woods toward the campus.

The students edged closer to the bonfire. It was evident something was about to happen. But what? No one knew for sure, but given what had been happening to some of their fellow dorm students in past days, they decided they were probably safer out here by the fire than in their pitch-black rooms.

"Let's just stay out here and talk," Fabian suggested to Michel.

Even as they spoke, they could see movement beyond the bonfire's light. At first, they thought it was animals attracted by the fire, edging in from the forest fringe. Later they would realize it was the president's DSP forces moving in en masse to surround and secure the campus.

Midnight came and went and nothing happened.

The group began to shrink. Some decided there was no danger after all and went inside, intending to put in some study time by candlelight. Others just wanted to go to bed.

"I've been out here since before dawn this morning," Michel reminded Fabian. "I'm very tired. I think I'll go in and get some sleep."

But curiously, every time Michel made an attempt to leave the fire, someone else engaged him in conversation.

Suddenly, the blackness of the night was shattered by the sound of terrified screams. The students heard the solitary screams of "*Au secours!* Help!" all over the campus. Then, silence.

"What a night! What a night!" Michel exclaims. "Everywhere, men and women were being massacred. People ran in and out of buildings. Those running in ran to their doom. We didn't know it then, but the soldiers were wearing masks and infrared helmets. They could see the students coming and were there waiting for them."

Some from the bonfire crowd ran to investigate. They found the hallways of the buildings literally running with blood. It came from the dormitory rooms where students—some already asleep in their beds—had been brutally and cold-bloodedly murdered.

No shot was fired in the wholesale massacre. The victims went silently—either stabbed in the throat or the back of the neck or by having the top of their skull zipped open with one quick slice of a knife to expose the brain. It was a noiseless procedure, evidenced only by the torrents of blood that ran everywhere.

Seeing the carnage, those who had gone to investigate ran for their lives. Some on the upper floors jumped from windows and died in the fall. Others broke arms and legs.

Amazingly, one or two of the victims escaped, even though their skulls had been peeled back and their brains exposed. They managed to stagger outside, hands to head, blood gushing everywhere. Later they would tell how their would-be murderers had warned, "If you don't want to follow the rules of the president, this is what you can expect."

They also told of soldiers entering the room and uttering the word "*Lititi?*"

"I didn't know what it meant," one survivor said. "I didn't know what to answer, but someone on the other side of the room answered, "*Mboka.*" The guard told him, "*Allez...go.*"

Only the DSP and other members of Mobutu Sese Seko's Ngbandi tribe understood what the secret passwords meant. To make the proper reply indicated you were one of them; to answer any other way was to die.

As the horror was revealed, it became crystal clear to the students outside that the DSP was on a deadly mission to annihilate them. If they wanted to live, they had to get away, but with agents everywhere, they knew their chances for escape were slim. Still, they had no choice. To stay was definitely to die.

So they ran.

Michel and Fabian took off together, racing toward the dense forest wilderness that bordered the east side of the university—the same woods through which soldiers had been seen earlier in the evening moving toward the campus.

As Michel ran for his life, he told himself there was always the hope that, by some miracle, the soldiers' bullets would miss them. And indeed, all around, the brothers could hear the thud of bullets striking the trees as they ran.

They pushed deep into the dense forest, ignoring the dangers that lurked in the blackness and the wild animals that inhabited its depths. They could hear others around them—fellow students, they hoped—crashing through the brush. Occasionally, there was a cry of pain as someone ran into a sharp branch or fell on the uneven ground.

Later, they would learn that some students ran in the opposite direction, hoping to find safety and refuge at the FAZ military camp. Instead, they found the regular army units had been transferred out. Others ran straight for the Zambian border with nothing but the clothes on their backs. Still others tried to stand and fight. One young man had his throat cut and his skull zipped open, yet survived and was able to get away.

Michel and Fabian spent the night deep in the forest, lying motionless on the cold, damp ground, hands clasped tightly, hearts thundering with fear and exhaustion. Every leaf that shook brought a fresh wave of terror.

About 4:00 in the morning, the two ventured out of their hiding place and cautiously made their way back to the university campus. Their intention was to collect their belongings and see in the light of day what had happened the night before.

It wasn't until they got inside the buildings that they realized the full extent of the carnage.

There were no bodies in the dormitories. Those had already been spirited away, taken to the hospital morgue where no one would be allowed to see or count them. But the blood remained—congealed in nauseating rivers in the hallways, in clotted stains running down walls from one floor to the other, mingling with clothing and food stashes in the rooms.

"It is hard to say how many died that night," Michel says. "Probably 400 or more. We estimate there were about 1,000 soldiers. Their mission was to finish off the students in the shortest time possible. It was obviously well planned because some students were given the secret password. Those who knew it were spared. Everyone else was a target."

The University of Lubumbashi did not open again. The doors were chained shut and many of the buildings were set on fire to destroy the evidence.

The government suppressed the story of the massacre. It was simply a small altercation, they reported, a tribal dispute between a couple of students who stabbed each other to death.

But the students knew the truth. They were survivors of a brutal, calculated, cold-blooded massacre and they were determined that the world should know about it.

So once again, the young people began organizing. Their recent experience gave new momentum to their UDSP party as the existing membership was joined by other survivors, some wounded students who had reached the hospital on their own or received first aid treatment from the university's Department of Medicine.

Conditions in Lubumbashi deteriorated even further after the massacre. An 8:00 evening curfew was imposed. Security forces were everywhere, paying specific attention to the homes of university students. Family members became fearful for their own lives and were reluctant to leave their dwellings.

Students who hailed from outside of Lubumbashi became virtual refugees in the city. Unable to travel and not daring to go to the government for assistance, many ended up destitute, sleeping on the streets and begging for food. Some tried to escape to neighbouring Zambia. A number were aided by Catholic priests and other Christian missionaries who had a premonition the worst was yet to come.

Students who lived in Lubumbashi were monitored closely. If two or three were seen talking together, they were ordered to go back home and never speak about what happened.

The demand just made the students more determined to go public with what had taken place at the university. The bitterest pill of all was hearing over and over in the media how the conflict was a trivial thing between one or two students. Somehow, they told one another, they had to let people know the truth.

But speaking out had its hazards. Many of the wounded who were taken to hospital had already been effectively silenced, murdered in their hospital beds, so they could never speak out.

Parents of missing students started asking authorities, "Where is my child?" They were warned, "Don't ask or what happened to your child will happen to you."

Michel and Fabian felt relatively secure within the guarded walls of the Lwamba family compound, but their mother Edwine was terrified. She knew her sons were determined to testify publicly about the massacre and she begged her husband to stop them.

Gilbert was as much aware as his wife that he could end up losing both his sons if they followed through with their plan, but he also understood their zeal and desperation to see the truth revealed.

"This is your country," he told them, "yours and your children's. I know, as you do, someone has to be willing to speak out and fight for it. If you feel you are the ones to do it, I won't forbid you because I did the same thing in years past. All I ask is that you be careful."

Turning to his wife, he continued in the parable style he favoured. "Edwine, if you see an old man putting flour in his mouth, it means he has enough saliva to wet it. In other words, he's man enough to do what is necessary." To Michel and Fabian he said, "If you two are men enough to do what is right, then go ahead."

Edwine continued to plead with her sons. "You escaped this tragedy because God did not want you to die," she said. "Please don't say anything. I couldn't bear to lose you."

Her plea touched Fabian and Michel deeply and they agreed to remain silent, even though they were both anxious to make the truth known.

And, indeed, as time went on, they found it harder and harder to keep the promise to their mother, especially when it became evident that whispers of the university massacre had spread beyond Zaire to the foreign press.

Belgium Radio, the BBC and other international media investigated, all wanting to know if there was truth to the massacre rumour. Amnesty International declared that they were looking for students willing to speak out about what had occurred at the University of Lubumbashi on May 9, 1989.

And so, despite their vow to their mother, Michel and Fabian volunteered to go with a number of other massacre survivors to tell their story to the world. While they hated going back on their word to their mother, they didn't want to be cowards, either.

Mobutu appeared to have no problem with the plan. He arranged for a number of media locations to be set up across the country where the students could go and tell their tale. He even issued calls on national television inviting anyone who knew anything about the "so-called massacre" to feel free to share their story at the prearranged venues. But behind the scenes, the DSP was dispatched to the homes of university students to use intimidation tactics to ensure no one would make an appearance. The authorities were confident they had everything in hand.

They were wrong.

More than 400 students showed up, many of them mobilized by Michel and Fabian Lwamba. All 400 were ready and eager to testify in front of Amnesty International and the world media.

The government's proposal was to have each person go individually into a special room to testify. Wisely, the students refused. They knew it was dangerous enough just being seen in the building. The whole event was being taped by video cameras, as was the student demonstration outside. Since they already had the ear of the government, some of the students decided to capitalize on the opportunity to bring up another important issue—the fact that their educational records had been frozen with the closure of the university. They demanded the government re-open the University of Lubumbashi so they could continue with their education.

One of the first students to speak to the assembled media was a young man named Likaya. He came wearing a hat.

"The government says nothing happened," Likaya scornfully declared as he stood to address the crowd. "Look..." He pulled off his hat, revealing where the top of his skull had been carved away. "I am one of the victims of the massacre. I am half dead already. I won't be going back to school." He pointed an accusing finger at the government officials present. "You have killed me!" he cried. "My life is over! Why don't you just bury me now?"

Tears were running down Likaya's face and down the faces of his listeners. The visual evidence of his testimony shocked and sickened everyone there and it stiffened the resolve of his fellow students who could hardly wait to add their own incriminating testimony. "At last," they told themselves, "the people of Zaire and the world would hear the truth."

With each testimony, the gathered international representatives added their voice to the students' to demand accountability from Mobutu and his regime.

The president's response was to halt the hearings immediately.

The students were devastated, yet encouraged by the support they were receiving from the outside world. It motivated them to keep up their pressure on the government and despite the overt threats and harassment, they kept up their demonstrations.

In late 1991, the people of Zaire were given another reason to protest. A national conference was arranged where the citizens of Zaire could come and express their views on the government's performance and articulate ideas for effective change. Once more, citizens streamed to the conference hall. Once more, after one day of hearings, the president closed it down.

Once more, outraged UDSP members prepared for another march of protest to the office of the governor who had finally agreed to meet with them and hear their grievances.

The march began as scheduled and suddenly—out of nowhere, it seemed—the old Congolese flag from the heady independence days of Patrice Lumumba appeared above the crowd. The flag belonged to Gilbert Lwamba and Fabian was carrying it above the marching demonstrators as a standard for freedom.

"We went down the street, waving the flag, demonstrating for our right to freedom, demonstrating for the university to open its doors again so we could go back to school," Fabian recalls, "and demonstrating to tell the government it had no right to kill students just because they wanted to make their views known. The flag stood for the days our father used to talk about—the days gone by when things were so much better. We wanted those times back again. We wanted change."

Raising the illegal Congolese flag was just one more strike against the Lwamba family, which had been in the sights of authorities for some time now. The president was personally displeased with the way Gilbert Lwamba had constantly opposed his policies and refused to support any official directives he considered to be wrong or inhumane. Thus, the president's people were keeping a wary eye on Gilbert's sons.

They were already well acquainted with George, who in his college days had been an outspoken proponent for justice and democracy. Now they were contending with Michel and Fabian who had apparently taken up the democratic torch.

"What was it about this family?" officials wondered. "Did these descendants of the African royal line have political ambitions? Were they secretly mobilizing to overthrow the president?"

Michel and Fabian were oblivious to the speculation as they led the singing marchers through the streets of Lubumbashi toward the governor's mansion. They were elated that the governor had finally agreed to meet with them.

The crowd swelled as it moved along. Young people, attracted by the singing, joined the march. Most had no idea what it was about, but they, too, picked up the chant, "We need change! We need change!"

The president's special security people were keeping a close eye on things and viewed the proceedings with much less benevolence. Just the fact that these students dared to demonstrate publicly after all the warnings they had received was infuriating enough. Then the old Congolese flag came into view.

It was the flash point for action.

The order was issued to stop the march.

The DSP stepped in and began pushing the crowd back.

The students resisted. "The governor is waiting to talk to us," they protested.

"If you have something to say, write it down and we'll give it to him," the soldiers replied.

The students refused. They had reached the edge of the governor's compound by now and could see him inside.

"We mean to speak to the governor in person. He said he would see us and we know he will listen because he attended our university. He was once a student. He will understand. Stand aside and let us go in and talk to him."

In retrospect, Michel says, the governor probably had no intention of talking to the students at all. "He was just playing a game. He promised to see us, but no doubt he had instructed the security people not to let us in."

As the students and soldiers shouted back and forth, the contention between the two groups intensified. The governor, perhaps alarmed by how large and boisterous the crowd had become, announced his intention to leave.

That made the students all the more adamant. "We must speak to the governor!" they shouted. "And we will!"

"Back off!" the soldiers ordered. They began counting. "One...two...three," and without warning, they turned their machine guns on the students and opened fire, spraying bullets indiscriminately into the crowd.

The air was soon filled with tear gas.

Chaos erupted.

The flag of democracy fell to the ground and many died that day. Not just students. Curious onlookers who had simply come to join the singing marchers were killed, too.

Everyone took off running.

"It was a terrible day," Fabian recalls, shaking his head sadly. "I truly believed that I would never see Michel again."

Chapter Five

MICHEL TOOK OFF RUNNING AS SOON AS THE TEAR GAS AND THE SHOOTING began. He headed straight for the Lwamba family compound.

He wasn't looking for protection; he knew things had gone far beyond that. As president of the student political movement and organizer of the demonstration, he was a prime target for Mobutu's DSP troops. The Lwamba mansion would be the first place the soldiers would come looking for him. Anyone they found would most likely be butchered on the spot or arrested.

His basic instinct was to get everybody out of the house as quickly as possible.

Michel figured he had a half-hour head start. After that, the soldiers would have learned his identity and figured out where to find him.

He arrived at the mansion, his T-shirt torn and soaked with perspiration, to find the house virtually empty. Only 13-year-old Aliston was at home with their young sister Gisele and Michel's daughter Sakina, who was barely two. Aliston had just come home from a soccer game. Everyone else, including Gilbert and Edwine and Michel's wife Betty, were out.

To his credit, Aliston didn't waste time asking questions when Michel burst into the house demanding they all leave immediately. He knew about the problems at the university and the fact that students had been killed. It didn't surprise him that there was more trouble.

Quickly, he helped his older brother gather up the two little girls who were playing outside in the compound.

They had to move quickly. It was only a matter of time before the soldiers would seize some students and beat or maybe even torture them until they revealed who the leader of the student movement was. Someone would say, "Michel Lwamba is the president and his younger brother Fabian is in charge of recruiting members. All their friends are involved, too." The authorities could easily corroborate that because they had the videos. They would see the brothers leading the march and Fabian holding the flag.

Michel knew his parents and Betty would be frantic when they found the two little girls missing, but he didn't have a choice. If any of them were to be spared, they had to disappear immediately.

He scooped up Sakina and set out on foot, running quickly between the houses to a nearby Catholic church. It was a big church and even though the Lwambas were not practising Catholics, Michel knew it was the safest place to go. Earlier, after the massacre at the university, the priests and people from other Christian ministries had been most generous in helping students get back to their families. Michel could only hope those same priests had heard about the demonstration and the killing that had just taken place in front of the governor's mansion and would be willing to help him.

It was 6:00 when they reached the church. One of the priests was in the process of locking the front door for the night when Michel and Aliston raced up.

"Please, please," Michel begged, "you have to let us in."

The priest took in Michel's dishevelled appearance, his torn clothing and the desperation in his eyes. He opened the door a bit.

"We're in serious trouble," Michel told him. "You probably heard about the demonstration this afternoon and the killings. Well, I just escaped death out there on the street, but if they catch me, I'm a dead man and none of my family will be spared. Please, we are begging you for refuge...."

The priest hesitated. "You are one of the students?"

"Yes, I am. If they find me, they'll kill me. These are the only family members that were at my home—everyone else was gone. I don't know where my father is....I don't know where my wife is....Please help us, if you can. Please spare our lives."

Still, the priest hesitated. "What am I to do?" he puzzled aloud. "If the soldiers find you hiding here, they'll kill all of us. But I can't send you away. If I do, you will most certainly die."

He opened the door wide enough to let the four slip inside. Then he closed and bolted it behind them.

He led the little group downstairs to a secret basement room.

"Do you think anyone saw you come here?" the priest asked.

Michel shook his head, hoping desperately it was true.

"Then stay here and be very quiet," the cleric warned them. "Don't say a word."

He closed the door and left.

The four huddled together.

Michel's head and his heart were pounding. What if someone had seen them? Would they tell the authorities? Where were Betty and their new baby boy Rodrigue? Where were his parents Gilbert and Edwine? Were they safe? And what about his beloved brother Fabian...?

The priest brought food to the basement room, but Michel was too worried to eat. Nor could he sleep when night came.

There was a small radio in the room and he turned it on just loud enough to hear the reports of the day. His heart sank when he heard his own name coming across the airwaves. "Authorities are looking for Michel Lwamba. He is wanted by police. Anyone knowing his whereabouts is ordered to get in touch with the police."

Michel found it very frightening to hear his name announced publicly on the radio. Oh God, he thought, what if someone did see me and they find us here? He was more convinced than ever that he and Aliston and the girls needed to get as far away as possible from Lubumbashi. But how? One step outside this little basement room would surely mean death for every one of them.

He was still awake when the door opened sometime during the night. A different priest entered the room.

"I hope you realize I am risking my life in doing this," he said to Michel, "but because of the little girls, I will try to get you across the border and out of Zaire. If we are caught, we will all die, but sometimes we have to give ourselves for other people." He motioned toward the door. "Come on. Let's go."

Under the cover of night, the priest led Michel, Aliston and the two girls through the darkened church and out a side door to a small panel truck with an enclosed box on the back. The box was normally used for hauling livestock; now the floor was covered with mattresses.

The priest helped them inside, then closed the door quickly and locked it.

Michel held his breath as the man got behind the wheel and switched on the ignition. He was still holding his breath as the wheels began to roll.

He had no idea in which direction they were heading. The only sound he could hear was the noise of the motor and the tires on the road.

They drove for a long time.

Fear made him distrust everything, even the unfamiliar priest who was driving the truck. Where exactly was he taking them? And what if he was actually someone sent by the government? Maybe they were being taken straight to President Mobutu.

When the truck slowed and finally came to a stop, Michel's heart was in his throat. "This is it," he told himself. "This is where we are going to be killed." He braced himself for the inevitable.

But nothing happened. They were only stopping for fuel.

Eventually, the vehicle reached the border. Michel found himself praying, "Please, God, don't let them stop us."

"I don't know how we got across without the authorities checking the truck," Michel says today, "but we did. And it's a good thing, too, because our pictures were posted everywhere. I believe the reason we weren't discovered was because the border guards had a habit of letting people from the church move back and forth quite freely. They respected them and probably didn't believe they would be doing something like this."

When the guard asked the purpose of the trip, the priest said he was heading for Nairobi, Kenya, for ecclesiastical purposes and that he had nothing in the back to declare except some used hymnbooks that he was taking to a Nairobi parish.

Throughout the whole ordeal, Michel was terrified that little Sakina would give them away. Only two years old, tired, bewildered and hungry, she looked ready to cry. Amazingly, she did not.

"When God wants to save you," Michel observes, "He does miraculous things."

Even now, Michel and Aliston aren't sure which route their driver took to Kenya, whether it was through Zambia or Tanzania. All they know is they drove for a very long time. There were brief stops for fuel and washrooms, but Michel didn't ask where they had stopped and made sure everyone was back inside the truck box as quickly as possible. On one occasion, he noticed English signs which indicated they were no longer in French-speaking Zaire. Further along, Aliston saw Swahili signs during a bathroom break, which was a clue they were probably travelling through Tanzania.

It was a relief to know they were out of Zaire, but Michel still didn't feel safe. He knew anything could happen at any moment. There was every possibility their whereabouts were known and they were being pursued. Any minute now, the pursuers might catch up.

The Lwambas spent most of the four day journey sleeping, cushioned on the mattresses and covered up. From time to time, the driver would slip some food inside the truck box for them.

Eventually, they reached Kenya and its capital, Nairobi.

The priest drove directly to United Nations headquarters where he explained the Lwambas' situation to the personnel there. He spoke in English, a language in which the brothers were only marginally fluent. Whatever he said made an impact because the UN people immediately began the process of registering the four as refugees. They were assigned a hotel room and given a requisition for the provisions they would need to live for the next few days.

After seeing Lwambas safely to their hotel room, the priest went out to get the food which he brought back to the room.

"He tried to encourage us and cheer us up," Aliston recalls, "but it didn't do much good. The food tasted like a sponge in our mouths and we ate with tears running down our faces. The more he tried to cheer me up, the more I cried. I was only 13; I was missing my mother. We were in a strange country, among strange people, and our lives had been turned upside down. Everything familiar was taken from us—our parents, our friends, our school. I didn't know what was going to happen to us."

The priest who drove them to safety had become their anchor in the midst of a very stormy and turbulent sea. They didn't know his name or his place of origin, but because he spoke both English and French fluently, the brothers believe he may have been from Eastern Canada. When the time came for him to leave, the little group could hardly bear to let him go.

"He had become like our own father," Michel says, "but he had to return to Zaire."

The four were left alone, penniless, abandoned in a strange country, frightened, with nowhere to turn. The hopelessness of the situation began playing more tricks on Michel's mind. He felt he could trust no one. Even the generosity of the UN people became suspect.

His life, which had been so privileged and secure to this point, was on the brink of disaster. He was on the run with his siblings and his little daughter, but he didn't know where they were going. He had no idea what was ahead. Nor did he know where his wife was. Or his father. Or his mother. Or his brother, Fabian. His best guess was that they were all dead by now.

"Why is it," he asked himself, "that I survived? Is this what I was born for? Why am I not dead, like the others, and forgotten?"

From those sentiments, his mind would invariably shift to his political endeavours. "I am a fugitive now, hiding to save my life because of what I believed in," he would reason with himself. "Does this mean I was completely wrong? I thought we were doing something positive....Why, oh why, didn't I listen to my mother?"

The United Nations issued Michel and his little family the necessary protection papers which enabled them to stay in Kenya, but the security of them gave no comfort. They ate their meals crying, wondering about and lamenting for the rest of their family.

As difficult and hopeless as the situation seemed, Michel and Aliston had no way of knowing things were about to get a whole lot worse.

The Lwambas were only four among tens of thousands of refugees that were streaming into Nairobi. Kenya was overrun by people fleeing for their lives from Somalia, Sudan, Zaire, Burundi and Angola. Victims of war and violence from their respective countries, they were all looking for a safe haven.

To this point, Kenya had only one refugee camp. Known as Thika, the camp was located within the capital of Nairobi. Thika could not begin to accommodate all the desperate people seeking asylum. Within a short time, the city's population became double that in the rest of the country.

Understandably, the Kenyan government was alarmed. How were they going to provide for all these people? The city was bulging at the seams, full to overflowing with desperate and needy people. It did not fit well with Nairobi's image as a tourist destination. Since tourism has always been a significant part of the Kenyan economy, it seemed a good idea to get the masses of refugees out of sight and as far away from the capital as possible.

The refugees were sent away arbitrarily, according to their refugee claimant file number. The files were arranged in stacks; 20,000 went to this camp, the next 20,000 to another.

The Lwambas were assigned to Kakuma, a refugee camp located two days' drive from Nairobi in the north-west corner of the country, near its border with Sudan. The camp was administered by Lutheran World Relief in conjunction with the United Nations High Commission on Refugees.

Michel had heard about refugee camps. He didn't know if he could bear to live in one. It was hard to accept that mere days ago he lived in the midst of wealth and privilege. Now all he had were the clothes on his back and the sobering responsibility of a brother and two little girls—plus the constant anxiety of knowing he was a hunted man.

It was a long bus ride to Kakuma. Michel, Aliston and the girls arrived at the camp around 5:00 in the morning.

Before leaving Nairobi, they had been shown a video of Kakuma, but nothing could have prepared them for the sight that met their eyes that morning in 1991. As the bus crested a hill, they could see the camp spread out below them. It looked like a gigantic hole in the earth, in the midst of a very flat, dry and windy plain.

The camp was actually located on a site where the indigenous Turkana tribes had buried their dead for generations. In fact, in Turkana the name "kakuma" means "dry bones." To Michel's mind, it was entirely appropriate. The terrain had a distinct look of death and devastation.

The camp itself was a sea of makeshift tent shelters. Situated in the middle of nowhere, Kakuma had one "street" that led north to the Sudanese border just a few kilometres away.

Though it was only 5:00 in the morning, the temperature was already extremely high.

The new refugees were sent to the camp's reception area to wait. There they listened to a speech informing the gathered newcomers that conditions in the camp would not always be as primitive as they appeared at the moment. Houses would soon be built.

Looking around him, Michel couldn't help wondering what those houses would be like. He suspected they would probably be nothing more than a plastic sheet stretched over some poles. He wondered how the Kenyan government could condone forcing people to live in a place like this. It was bone dry. There wasn't a stick of vegetation in the camp and no water source. Michel had no idea how they were expected to survive in such conditions.

In Nairobi, he had perceived the Kenyans to be clean and tidy people, but there was nothing clean or tidy about Kakuma.

There were indigenous Turkana peoples who fit a typical primitive African stereotype. The Turkanas shunned clothing and even for native Africans like Michel and Aliston, it came as a shock to see people walking around naked.

The Turkanas did not want the refugees in their territory. The newcomers did not speak English, the official language of the country, nor did they share the same value system as the Turkanas where killing was a way of life. If they wanted something, they simply took it.

The camp's population was loosely grouped into communities according to their country of origin. Michel and his family were assigned to a community made up of refugees from Zaire. The Zairean sector numbered about 100 adults, plus children. Some were students who had fled the massacre in Lubumbashi; others were from Kinshasa. Still others had come to Kenya simply hoping to escape Mobutu's brutal and corrupt regime.

Rather than feeling safe among people from his own country, Michel's anxiety increased. He lived with the possibility that at any moment the Zairean next to him might learn his identity and turn him in for the reward being offered for his capture. Like most refugees, he quickly learned to identify himself only by his first name.

The Lwambas were issued a blue plastic bag and some poles to make a dwelling for themselves. Family-sized bags created a three-metre square tent shelter. Individual refugees were given smaller bags that covered a one- to two-metre square area, but they were expected to share the space with at least one other person.

The plastic bag shelter provided little in the way of privacy or security, particularly at night when lions often entered the camp and roamed about looking for food. Very often it was the refugees who became their prey.

Because of its location in the camp, the Zairean sector was in a constant danger zone. The Zaireans had about 2,000 Ethiopian militaries living beside them. These displaced Ethiopians had escaped to Kenya when their side lost the country's civil war. Now the soldiers spent their days in the camp with guns loaded, ready to resist the frequent and inevitable attempts of the current Ethiopian government to kidnap them and take them back for punishment. The kidnap raids always involved shooting and violence that caught many innocent people—often children—in the crossfire.

Adding to the danger, the camp was bracketed by two warring Turkana tribes. Both were primitive peoples who had inhabited the drought-stricken area for centuries. They solved their water shortage problems by drinking the blood of their cattle. As a result, the perimeter of the camp was strewn with the rotting carcasses of dead cows. It created an indescribable stench and was a constant attraction for disease-carrying insects and predatory wild animals.

The two tribes existed in constant conflict. Though they clung to their primitive lifestyle, they had modern weaponry that they used almost nightly in disputes over cows, camels, donkeys and anything else that one tribe wanted from the other.

The refugee camp, and the Zairean area in particular, was vulnerable to the clashes. Almost every night, someone in the Zairean community died. In fact, the day the Lwambas arrived in Kakuma, while they were still in the reception area, a woman was struck by gunfire from one of the warring sides and died. For Michel and Aliston, it was a rude introduction to life in the camp.

Kakuma also served as a military base for Sudanese rebel soldiers, entering for medical treatment and leaving when they were able to rejoin their units. Their presence was a continual reminder of the horrors of war.

"One day you would see a man walking around normally on two legs," Michel recounts. "The next day you would see him with only one leg. What happened? He was a rebel soldier who went across the border to Sudan, got involved in the fighting and has come back without a leg.

"You wonder: How can he go and fight when no guns are allowed in camp? The answer is simple. Even though the UN and the Government of Kenya don't officially allow guns in refugee camps, they are still present. The UN knows it, but they don't say anything because they know Kakuma was a Sudanese rebel camp before it was a refugee camp. And they don't confiscate the artillery because they know the Sudanese are only there temporarily and will go back to the fighting in their own country as soon as they can."

Still, having the armed Sudanese as neighbours impacted every aspect of life in the refugee camp. No one dared to anger them in any way, especially in the food lines.

"These rebels are very, very aggressive and their tempers are at the flash-point," Michel explains. "They have seen a lot of bloodshed and they are desperate people. They know that at any minute they may be kidnapped and taken prisoner, so they live in the moment. They make sure they have what they need for whatever period of life they have left. And what they want, they get."

Another hazard for refugees was natural dangers, like scorpions and tarantula-sized spiders whose deadly bite crazed the victim's mind; poisonous snakes and insects that attacked cows, camels and humans and whose bite could bring on sleeping sickness, typhoid or malaria.

Then there were wild animals.

Shortly after coming to Kakuma, Michel had an encounter that could have cost his life. One morning, he got up very early and headed for the bushes that served as the camp's latrine. He did not know that in the early morning hours, wild animals lurked near the settlement.

On this particular morning, he ran into a whole family of very large chimpanzees.

"It is a miracle I wasn't attacked," he says. "With a group like that, if you have anything that attracts their attention—whether it's a cup or a shiny button—they can jump on you and tear you to pieces."

Adding to the physical perils were their personal anxieties. Gisele had sickle cell disease that made her chronically ill and resulted in a lot of pain.

Gisele's medical treatment called for at least one cup of milk a day, but there was no milk to be had in Kakuma.

The nearest water was a two-hour walk away. It came from a well dug by UNICEF several years before. Now the water was full of salt, but it was all they had.

Michel soon learned the daily routine of getting up very early and carrying the water container on the long trek to and from the well. Every day was a challenge. With wild animals all along the way, it was everyone for himself.

Making the journey even more difficult was the fact that the savannah land through which they traversed was overgrown with thorns. Walking was treacherous and the continuous searing wind was laden with sand that bit into the flesh. Balancing a jerry can of water on the head prevented the bearer from turning his face away from the punishing blast. It would take several years before the damage to Michel's eyes from the driven sand was completely healed.

Every Friday, more refugees from all over Africa were dropped off at Kakuma Camp and as the population exploded, UNICEF decided the two-hour walk for water was unacceptable. Too many people were dying by the wayside. Another water pipe was installed much closer to the camp, only a half-hour's walk away. It was a tremendous relief for the refugees, but as the camp grew to 150,000 and then to 200,000, water lineups became longer and longer. Refugees were forced to get up earlier and earlier.

"And still," Michel says, "there were those who came late and pushed you out of the line to take your place, even though you were there much earlier."

The same thing happened in the food lineups on Distribution Day.

Food distribution took place once every two weeks. The regimen was inflexible and merciless. Missing Distribution Day meant waiting two more weeks for food rations.

In order to receive a ration, each person had to show a food ration card. If the card was lost or stolen, no food would be given. The person either found a card or waited until another one was issued.

Even then, rations were sparse and the amounts became smaller and smaller as the number of refugees increased. Food was trucked in and waiting recipients always faced the possibility that the food convoy might be hijacked.

That happened shortly after the Lwambas arrived in Kakuma. Bandits hijacked the UN trucks and stole all the foodstuffs. The entire camp was forced to share whatever rations they had left and wait for the next load of humanitarian food aide.

When the Lwambas first arrived at the camp, they were given a speech describing the type of food they could expect to receive. The description came nowhere near reality. Rations for each person were two cups of dry beans, a half cup of sugar, salt to fill a Coke bottle cap and some rice and oil.

Eating was a discipline. Even when the food got through, the ration amounts were too small for two meals a day for everyone, so Michel limited himself to one meal so there would be enough for the three younger ones. He made it through each day consoling himself with the knowledge that he would be able to eat in the evening.

"You thought about every mouthful you ate," he says. "There was no such thing as breakfast. I found if I ate once or twice in two days and had a drink of water, I could stretch the rations and survive. But it was hard. All around us, people were starving to death, but sharing even a glass of water was a sacrifice too great to make."

Lineups on Distribution Day were a mad crush, as people on the verge of starvation tried to force their way nearer to the front of the line. It was not uncommon for people to be knocked to the ground and trampled to death. Often, it was children who died this way.

"You wanted to stop and help, but you didn't dare or you would lose your own place in the food line," Michel says. "And you couldn't miss out on getting food because your own family needed it. Food, food, food—everything centred around getting enough food."

Adding to the stress of Distribution Day were the security guards who felt no regret whatsoever about using clubs to keep the crowd in check. Many people ended up receiving medical attention after being beaten by the guards, instead of receiving their precious food allotment for which they would now have to wait another two weeks.

An American organization known as the International Rescue Committee (IRC), in co-operation with Médecins Sans Frontières (Doctors Without Borders), operated a small infirmary in the camp. Its primary purpose was to treat Sudanese war casualties, but refugees also depended on it for medical treatment.

Michel became a nurse in the clinic, something he finds sadly amusing in retrospect. "Being a political science student, you wouldn't expect I could do much," he says, "but I was considered one of the best. You can imagine what the rest of the hospital helpers were like. There were very few properly trained people. You received a few days of instruction and became a nurse."

Though Michel had witnessed his share of bloodshed and carnage, he had never seen anything like what he encountered in the little clinic—people dying of starvation and HIV/AIDS and the shocking casualties of the Sudanese war.

Many times he saw casualties carried into the camp from miles away. Some came on their own, directly from the fighting, which was a good three days' walk away. One young fighter brought his severed arm with him in a bag.

"It was an unbelievable sight," Michel says. "It had taken this man three days to walk to the hospital. By that time, the arm was stinking and the wound had gone three days without treatment. The whole time he walked, thinking there might be some way his arm could be reattached.

"I asked, 'What happened to your arm?' He said, 'It was chopped off by the enemy. I have it in this bag.' He took it out and I almost fainted. I had never seen anything like that before. What was I to do? I was no doctor. All I had was a quick training so I could check medications and hand them out.

"I said, 'I can't help you with this. They will have to transfer you to a hospital in the city, but they won't be able to do anything for that arm.' He wanted it fixed so he could go back to the war."

Another time, a young Sudanese man appeared at the hospital, his leg shattered from ankle to knee. He had a piece of cloth stuffed inside the wound and had bound the whole thing around with his shirt. Somehow the man made it back to the camp. The leg, of course, had to be amputated.

Epidemics constantly raced through the camp, aided by the unwaveringly hot conditions. Temperatures held steady at around 42°C (nearly 110°F). The abysmal conditions in the little hospital only contributed to the rampant spread of disease. There were about 50 single beds in the infirmary, but it wasn't uncommon to have 100 people needing treatment. The only way to handle the caseload was to put 2 in a bed, head to foot. Often the 2 would have different illnesses. One might be suffering from malaria, the other from diarrhea. Each one usually ended up with both diseases.

There was no electricity in the camp hospital and just one paraffin lamp.

"People died in the night all the time, but you couldn't do anything because there was only the one lamp," Michel recalls. "While you were helping one person, you would hear another screaming somewhere in the darkness because they had been bitten by a scorpion."

When Aliston contracted malaria, Michel told him it would be safer to stay in their little tent shelter and take the medicine he brought from the infirmary.

Michel believes it was only by a miracle of God that he stayed healthy in the refugee camp. It is all the more remarkable given the fact that Michel had lost considerable weight from limiting his own food and water intake so Sakina and Gisele could have more.

"I looked like a skeleton," he says, "but God protected me from all the diseases I was exposed to in the hospital. Many times diarrhea spread like an epidemic throughout the camp and the infirmary had to wait for medicine from Médecins Sans Frontières in Nairobi. The plane came once a week with medicines, but that was too long for many people."

It was a brand new, terrifying world for Michel. As he watched the population of the refugee camp grow and the mortality rate skyrocket, he often asked himself the haunting question: Why is all this happening to me?

Chapter Six

THE ISOLATION OF THE REFUGEE CAMP WAS ALTERED SOMEWHAT WHEN A GROUP of Canadians came to shoot a documentary film at Kakuma.

Because he could speak a little English, Michel was selected to interact with them. At the end of their stay, the Canadians gave him a small radio. "So you can listen to the news," they said, "and at least know what is going on in the rest of the world."

The radio became the Zairean community's sole link with the outside world and it was constantly surrounded by listeners eager to hear the BBC or Voice of America.

At one point, Michel happened to catch a French program from Radio Canada. It talked about the rich country that Canada was and the good education system it had. Michel vowed, if he ever had the opportunity, he would go to Canada. But from where he sat in the dirt of the refugee camp, such a thing seemed utterly impossible.

The BBC carried one daily program that focused on Central and East African matters. From the reportage, the refugees heard accounts of the ongoing fighting and massacres in their home areas.

"It only added to the burden on our hearts," Michel says. "We were already grieving and then we'd hear more bad news and even worse, have it confirmed by Radio International and Radio Canada. We got more depressed every day."

One day in particular, Michel was profoundly depressed. He had been thinking about his parents, his family, his life. He'd had nothing to eat that day because the truck bringing food was once again hijacked by poachers and now the camp population would have to wait another three weeks before the next food shipment came.

His heart was very heavy. "My daughter Sakina asked me for something to eat and I had nothing to give her. What could I say to her? How could I explain? Little children don't understand. All I could do was cry."

Michel was filled with fear for his little family. While he was at the hospital, it was Aliston's job to look after Gisele and Sakina. Michel was insistent the girls must never be left alone. Every day there were reports of children being kidnapped and raped.

The lower Michel's spirits sank, the more often he found himself turning to God to demand answers.

"What did I do to deserve this?" he asked. "Why am I here suffering? Why did You let this happen? Is this how everybody in my family is living now? Do I even have any family left?"

It wasn't that he expected an answer from God. For him, Christianity had always been some vague philosophy. He had heard about Jesus often enough in the church where he and his brothers used to go to hear the music, but all the talk of God got mixed up with his political ideologies and the usual philosophical questions: Should I remain a Muslim or become a Catholic? Or should I doubt all religion?

At university, he once heard a group of Christians singing and preaching about the need of every person to ask God's forgiveness for their sins and accept the way of salvation He prepared through Jesus Christ. Michel had decided to follow his father's counsel and just focus on living a decent life, doing good deeds.

Now, in his desperation, some of the things he'd heard in the Christian church in Lubumbashi were filtering back into his mind. He remembered hearing that the Bible said God would not permit anyone to be tempted or tried beyond their faith.

"This is already too much for me," he informed God. "I don't know where my father is, my mother, my brother, my wife....I have nothing. All our belongings and our houses have been confiscated by the government. All I have are these three kids and if something happens to me, what will become of them? What will happen to my little daughter? Who is going to take care of my brother? Who will bury me?"

Then came an event that would be a turning point for Michel and, in many ways, a transforming event for the entire Kakuma Refugee Camp. Michel recounts:

"I was out walking one night, trying to relax and clear my head of all the heavy, depressing thoughts. Sakina was with me. She was about seven at the time. We were walking slowly, hand in hand, when all of a sudden we were surrounded by people I didn't know. It seemed, though, that they knew me."

There were about 16 men, armed with knives and sticks. The knives they carried were distinct—curved blades worn around their wrists like a bracelet. The blade had a plastic cover so it wouldn't injure the wearer, but when it came time to fight, the cover was slipped back to expose a blade so lethal it could slice a person wide open in one sweep. The men surrounding Michel and Sakina had their blades open and ready for action.

"One could speak a little Swahili. He demanded I give them money. Apparently they knew I worked at the hospital and thought, as a 'doctor' in the clinic, I would have money. The truth was, I was paid 400 Kenyan shillings a month—about $10 to $15.

"It was Friday, which was usually payday, but this was a holiday so I wouldn't get paid until after the holiday was over. I said: 'I don't have any money.'"

The men began picking up stones.

Michel, dressed only in shorts, wrapped his arms around his daughter and held on tightly. He knew the two of them were completely defenceless.

"God," he prayed desperately, "this is it. There isn't anything I can do. I am surrounded by 16 men with knives and stones....I can't reason with them because they speak a language I don't understand and it is so dark I can't even recognize the face of the person throwing the stone. Oh my God, please help me."

At that point, a couple of the men tried to snatch Sakina out of Michel's arms, but he held on tight. He knew he would rather die than let his daughter be taken.

One man came at him with a wooden club and struck him a blow across the back of the shoulder hard enough to leave a permanent scar.

"Bring money," the attacker demanded.

"I have no money," Michel protested again, trying to fend off yet another man who was attempting to wrench the battered running shoes off his feet. All the while, others were pulling at Sakina's arms, trying to yank her out of his grasp.

"Daddy! Daddy!" she screamed. "Help me!"

There was nothing Michel could do but hold on tight—and pray.

"I said, 'Jesus, help me....' That's all I could do. There was no use screaming; we were too far from our community for anyone to hear. And besides, people knew when they heard a scream, it meant someone was being attacked and it was safer not to get involved because they could get killed, too."

The circle around Michel and his daughter tightened.

One man raised his arm to hurl the first stone.

This is it, Michel thought.

Another man grabbed his hand. "Don't throw the stone," he said. "This guy might scream and the police will come and arrest us."

Then, a very strange thing happened.

As Michel had prayed his desperate prayer, 'Jesus, help me,' he noticed a faint light in the distance. The light was rapidly approaching the spot where the menacing ring continued to encircle him. It soon became apparent that the light belonged to an approaching vehicle.

The attackers saw the lights, too, and not wishing to be recognized, they dropped their stones and ran. In the glare of the oncoming headlights, Michel recognized the man who had spoken to him in Swahili. He was someone Michel had cared for at the medical clinic.

The vehicle turned out to belong to the military police who were out patrolling the camp—something they rarely did. The soldiers arrived in time to see the fleeing men, but too late to go after them.

Michel explained all that had happened. "Thank God you came," he said. "Tonight would have been my last. I thought I was going to die."

The episode shook Michel to the very core of his being. That night, he had a long conversation with God.

"Thank you for saving me," he prayed. "I thought this was my last night. I looked left and right, forward and behind, and found no one to help. Then I looked up and You were there. I know now that You are my help."

As he closed his eyes, he saw what resembled a ribbon of fire connecting him with his Heavenly Father. It would be a recurring image, giving him comfort and the motivation to keep on in the hard days ahead.

Having encountered God in such a personal way, Michel began praying often and reading the Gideon Bible he had received when he first came to Kakuma. Everyone in the camp had a Gideon Bible. Some used the pages for toilet paper; others, for starting their cooking fires. Some used the fine paper for rolling cigarettes. One man joked that it was his way of getting the Word deeper inside of him.

As Michel studied the Bible and prayed, he began to think about the people who had tried to kill him and about his daughter's haunting question afterward: "Are these people not Christians, Daddy?"

Looking at his daughter now, seeing the bruises on her arms, remembering how close he had come to losing her and his own life, he was struck by the realization that the attackers were indeed desperate men who knew nothing of the love of God.

"They do things like this because they don't know You, God," he told his Heavenly Father. "Isn't there some way You can let these people know about Your love and hear Your Word?"

The request seemed paradoxical. Here he was in the midst of his own hopeless situation with no way out, no hope of a life beyond the camp. So why was he asking God to do something good for a group of strangers who tried to kill him?

Indeed, something had changed. Not the circumstances nor his prospects for the future, but Michel himself had changed. He felt different. He thought differently. He sensed an inner peace he had never had before.

"Even in my awful situation, God was able to comfort me," he says. "I didn't know it then, but He was showing me that even though I thought it was the end, it was really only the beginning.

"I definitely know it was God who spared my life that night," he adds. "Soldiers rarely patrolled the refugee camp. First, because they knew the Sudanese had guns. Second, because not long before, some soldiers were seized by the Sudanese and murdered. No one was in a hurry to be the next victim. But for that night, for whatever reason, God brought that military vehicle to show me that even though I was in an impossible situation, He could help me. I realized in that moment that He had always been there, watching over us and protecting us."

Michel was consumed with an inexplicable urge to gather the people in his community together and tell them what God had done, about Jesus and what the Bible said about Him. He wanted his fellow refugees to know that if they would only trust God then they, too, could be spiritually rescued and have the hope of heaven, rather than suffering eternity in hell.

He began to share this message with the people around him, but his audience wasn't particularly receptive. "We're already in hell," they countered. "That's all there is here—suffering and hell."

And it was true. Every person in the camp had a personal horror story to tell. Even the United Nations people who ran the camp were overwhelmed with tremendous stress from seeing everyone around them sick, suffering and dying, struggling to cope with many potentially fatal problems.

No one was listening and Michel realized his words weren't making a dent on the embittered souls of these people. Yet, he was learning to wait on God for direction and inspiration.

"God has many ways of dealing with people," he observes. "Sometimes He allows things to happen just so He can demonstrate that He is Almighty God, the King above all kings."

Michel went back to reading his Gideon Bible and growing closer to God through prayer. His faith steadily increased, as God's Holy Spirit helped him make sense of what he was reading. Truths he had never considered nor understood became dear to his heart. Things he had heard from Christians in his past, even the lessons his mother and father had taught him about doing good, flooded to his mind.

One thing in particular that his father used to say became a motto for his life: "Wherever you go, try to leave your mark. Just make sure it is a good mark so people will remember you for a good deed rather than a bad one."

It was the motivation Michel needed to inspire him to rally his fellow refugees. But what could he do? How could he reach people who were totally consumed with resentment and hatred toward those who had destroyed their lives, killed their families and taken everything that was precious to them? How was he going to tell them, "Jesus loves you....I know He does because I am in the same situation you are, but I am confident I will come out of this dark tunnel. I feel it inside me. I know I will be victorious, even if victory means going to be with Jesus in heaven when I die."

Teach them a song.

The thought came to his mind with urgent clarity.

Michel pondered the idea. He certainly understood the power of a song. How often had he known a melody, a phrase, a lyric line to linger in the mind for days, popping up at the most unlikely moments, even when he didn't want it to? And singing was definitely something he could do.

"We're going to write a song," Michel told Aliston, "and we're going to sing it at night when everyone is quiet. That's when things seem the darkest and most hopeless."

The brothers set to work and the very next night the two sang their song together in front of their tent. Their sweet harmony, honed from long hours of practising back home in Lubumbashi, carried across the night air.

Some people complained and told the brothers to be quiet. Others said, "How can these people sing in a place like this?"

But Michel and Aliston kept on writing new songs and singing. Before long, early in the mornings, they began hearing their own songs on the lips of other people.

All those years of creating new music with American-styled melodies and African rhythms had been an invaluable training ground, but the lyrics the boys were now writing were relevant to life in the refugee camp. Their songs grew out of the common experience of living day-to-day in the midst of deep sorrow and hardship.

One of their first songs was about a little child. It came from witnessing the way children in the refugee camp suffered, seeing them wake up in the morning crying for breakfast, crying for water, crying because they were sick and there was no medicine to help them.

The songs came out of their own experiences. One day Sakina said to her father, "Daddy, what are we doing here? When are we going home?" Michel had no answer. All he could do was grieve. Then he dried his tears and tried to answer her questions in a song.

"When we wrote the songs, we had no idea we would someday be singing them to audiences all over the world," he remarks. "At that time, we believed we would die in the refugee camp or that maybe someday, if peace ever returned to our country, we would go back home."

Another song the young men wrote was about God helping Noah. Still another spoke of those who cried out to kill Jesus, not realizing He was innocent and that He was on a mission to die for them.

"Jesus knew He was saving each one of those people who were screaming, 'Kill him, kill him, kill him,'" Michel says. "Every drop of blood that came from His hands cried out, 'I love you, I love you, I love you....'"

Michel wanted the words of the songs to be understood by everyone in the camp, but that presented a problem. In Zaire alone, there are more than 540 dialects, but the unifying language of the country is French. So each time he and Aliston wrote a new song, they wrote it first in French, then took it to others in the camp and asked them to translate it into their own peculiar dialect. At night, the singers would repeat the song in the various dialects so everyone within hearing range could understand what they were singing about.

When they sang a song called "Stop the Fight," listeners thought the Lwambas were trying to make a political statement. That gave Michel an opening to explain about Jesus and about loving one another, rather than hating the other person.

"Look at us," he would say. "We are in this camp because of hatred and war and misunderstanding. Some of the hatred has been going on for generations. Maybe together, you and I can do something deliberate to stop that cycle right now."

As they continued singing night after night, others gradually began to join in. They were a captive audience—occupants of a sea of tents spaced a mere five metres apart.

"We sang at night because that was when everything was quiet. Often people were awake, unable to sleep because they were thinking about their past and the hopelessness of their future. Night was when many people committed suicide," Michel says. "If we missed a night singing, there was sure to be someone who came the next morning and asked, 'Why didn't you sing last night? What happened? Were you sick? We missed your music. It keeps us going.'"

Gradually, people became more receptive. "Why do you sing these songs?" someone would ask. "You and your family are in the same situation we are. We're all starving to death, we are all under a sentence of death. How is it you can keep on singing?"

"It is Jesus," Michel would declare. "Jesus keeps me going. That is why I can close my eyes to the turmoil here and just focus on Him. I don't want to look back. If you keep looking back, you will never stop thinking about what's happened to you. I want to look ahead."

The message was simple, but it had a profound effect. People were willing to listen because they respected Michel. He had gained a reputation in the community for his peaceable behaviour and his trustworthiness. He had even been voted leader and spokesperson for the Zairean camp.

"I sometimes felt a little like Moses," Michel confesses, "especially when people would gather around and listen to everything I said. When there was a misunderstanding or a conflict between two or three refugees, God would give me the wisdom and the words to reason them out of the conflict and they would end up shaking hands and being friends again."

One of the places where people gathered was under Michel's cassava tree. Shortly after coming to the treeless camp, Michel planted a chunk of cassava root beside his tent. Cassava is a plant with starchy roots from which tapioca is obtained. Its leaves are edible, if cooked well, and nutritious. Nurturing the sapling meant sacrificing some of his precious water ration, but Michel did that and eventually the quick-growing sapling grew to be a tree with broad green leaves. It provided protection from the blistering sun, and people in the Zairean community gravitated to its shade. Michel used the opportunity to talk to those gathered about God and His goodness and love.

He did his best to live circumspectly in every aspect of camp life. He knew his fellow refugees were watching him carefully, quietly monitoring everything he did. When a problem arose, he would search the Scriptures for an answer. He freely acknowledged that any wisdom he had came from God and he would tell people, "Even though we may not all be Christians, the only way for us to get along here and be united is to follow what the Bible says."

Michel was constantly called upon to mediate situations that were perceived as life and death, but in any other circumstance would have been trivial. Possession of food and water, one person having a larger shelter than the other—all were crisis issues in the powder keg conditions of Kakuma. The accusation, "You ate twice in two days," was enough to provoke one person to stab another to death. In the blink of an eye, a stolen cup of water could erupt into a full-blown battle with knives drawn.

On one occasion, two men began fighting over some sugar on Distribution Day. One had stepped backwards and accidentally knocked over the other's cup of sugar. The second person pulled a knife and was ready to kill the first.

Michel intervened.

"Please," he told the aggressor, "don't kill this fellow over a cup of sugar. Here...." He handed the man his own cup of sugar.

Aliston, who was watching the altercation, gasped. "What are we going to do?" he asked his brother.

"I can't allow a man to lose his life over something as simple as a cup of sugar," Michel replied calmly. "We can live without it. In another month, we'll have sugar again."

The conflict ended, but Michel's actions had made a significant impact on observers. "Why would you do that?" they asked. "You aren't the one who spilled the sugar. What will happen to your own family? We know you have children to feed."

The incident prompted many to join with Michel and others who had begun gathering every Sunday to sing and pray together. Michel organized a choir and a couple of Christian men, one from Uganda and one from Congo, shared the preaching and Bible teaching with him.

During the gatherings, some would share what God was doing in their lives. Others confided their problems and anxieties. With death an imminent possibility every day, many asked the question, "What will happen to me when I die?" The assurance from the Bible that there is life in heaven with Jesus after death was indeed good news.

"It was the only hope they had," reflects Michel. "We preached hope through Jesus Christ. Instead of condemning people for what they were doing or had done wrong, we gave them hope in God and in heaven."

One Sunday, while singing in the little tent church with Michel, Aliston was overwhelmed with the desire to devote his life to Jesus Christ.

"Tears came to my eyes," he remembers, "and I cried and cried. I didn't know why I was crying. Maybe I felt sorry for myself. But soon my crying turned to crying out to God to help me. I knew He was the only one who could. That day I gave myself to Jesus. I began praying every day and soon I found myself waking up each morning singing and being really happy as I grew closer and closer to Jesus."

The congregation that was being established in Kakuma camp was all-inclusive. No tribe or person was excluded. Since not everyone spoke the same language, the services were conducted in French and translated into English.

"We believed it was very important to make this congregation open to everyone," Michel says, "because the Bible states that every knee shall bow down and every tongue will confess Jesus."

Zaireans, Sudanese, Ugandans, Ethiopians and even Kenyan United Nations employees began attending the Sunday gatherings. Many came out of curiosity. They wondered why people who were living on the same skimpy rations would deliberately deny themselves food in order to fast and pray. They soon learned it was because the Christians believed that without fasting and prayer they would never find the grace nor the power to forgive those who had so terribly wronged them.

"Forgiveness is a very difficult thing to do," Michel observes. "We had lived a privileged life. Now our family was slaughtered and everything we owned was gone. We were in this desert refugee camp, living in horrible conditions. We had been there for years, for reasons we didn't understand. In order for us to forgive the people responsible for all of that, we had to fast and pray.

"We did a lot of praying. Not only were we praying to forgive, we prayed that God would do a miracle and somehow make a way for us to get out of the camp. We fasted and prayed for all the countries that were troubled by bloody wars—not just Zaire, but the countries of virtually everyone living in the camp.

"We started out praying for ourselves, but then we realized that God already knew what we wanted. He saw where we were and He was watching over us. We didn't want to pressure Him, so we said, 'Let's forget about ourselves and address the real problems.' We began praying for other people—people we had never met. We prayed for nations and for Christians around the globe, for the servants of God who spend their time going out and preaching the Gospel.

"We prayed for the leaders of countries. We prayed for Mobutu, too. We prayed that God would touch his heart and make him realize the wrong he was doing. We prayed that Jesus would save him from evil. We had come to the point where we had forgiven the wrongs done to us and we did not want revenge, but in order to truly forgive him, we had to pray fervently and mean it deeply. We became genuine Christians in that place."

One United Nations man, Mr. Macomfrey, became a regular attendee at the camp church. Macomfrey was the UN employee in charge of distributing tents and shelters. He had chosen the Kakuma posting over working with a Christian organization in his native Finland. He made the choice because he wanted to avoid Christians.

But now, observing the way these Christians in Kakuma Camp were praying, despite their desperate circumstances, Macomfrey couldn't help but be impacted. After one service, he said to Michel, "I have been avoiding becoming a Christian. I ran away from Finland for that very reason, but I can see that the same Jesus I was running from is in this camp. What I have seen here makes me realize I want to be a Christian."

Refugees, seeing the UN officer on his knees, begging God to forgive him, said, "If this man can kneel here in the dirt and the sand and pray to become a Christian, so can we." And many did.

The Christians in Kakuma Refugee Camp began to see amazing answers to prayer. On one occasion, after a food convoy was hijacked and the camp was reduced to a state of near starvation, the Christians began praying for food. God answered in a most unusual way.

Kakuma is situated near the River Tarach, a water course that originates in Uganda, but is dry for most of the year. On rare occasions, when Uganda experiences torrential rain, the riverbed fills with water, which surges eastward into Kenya, resulting in flash floods.

One such flood occurred when the camp had been without food for two weeks. The refugees awoke one morning to find the riverbed flooded and alive with creatures leaping and moving in the water. When the torrent subsided, they discovered the river bottom was teaming with black mudfish—hundreds of them per square metre, enough to feed the entire camp for a whole month.

Incidences like this made Michel and his fellow believers all the more aware that God was with them and wanted to use them in the midst of an impossible situation.

The Scripture passage about God's people being put through the refiner's fire came to mind often in those days. Could it be, they wondered, that God was allowing them to go through this experience in order to refine them for His higher and better purpose?

The idea encouraged the believers and gave them the strength to persevere. They began calling the refugee camp their fire. If they endured patiently, they knew that somehow God would bring them forth shining, like purest gold.

Chapter Seven

MICHEL, ALISTON, GISELE AND SAKINA LWAMBA HAD BEEN IN KAKUMA Refugee Camp for about four years when another group of Canadians came to visit. This time, it was university students who were conducting a study on refugee camps as part of a college research project. Their format included inter-viewing individual refugees to find out why they had left their home country.

Once again, Michel was selected to speak with the students. He wasn't thrilled at the idea. First, he wasn't entirely sure the students were who they claimed to be, nor how much of his story it was safe to tell. If he told them he was once the leader of a student political movement in Zaire, he feared they might report him to the Mobutu government and he would be taken back to his home country.

Another concern was that the study group was using students from all over the world, not just Canada. What if the Zairean embassy had heard of their coming and contacted individuals, asking them to be on the lookout for "friends" or relatives in the refugee camp?

"Please," the official might have said, "let me know if you meet my cousin so I can go and visit him."

Michel knew full well the devious lengths to which his government was pre-pared to go to locate political refugees. On several occasions, Zaireans in Kakuma Camp were kidnapped and taken away because someone had inno-cently divulged their whereabouts.

Michel co-operated in the interview, but he remained vigilantly on guard. He described life in the refugee camp, but when it came to his personal story, he was much sketchier.

"I am a political refugee," he told the Canadians. "What brought me here is a very long story that I will never completely forget. There will always be a scar on my heart, but I have decided to forgive what happened so I can move on with my life."

The Canadians met Aliston and Gisele, as well as Michel's little daughter Sakina. They were particularly interested in the fact that the Lwambas were well educated and that Michel had a university degree. They sympathized with the Lwambas' circumstances, but that was about all they could do.

"We are only students," the young people said, "but perhaps we could try speaking to some embassies on your behalf to see if anybody is interested in resettling you."

The Canadians left and were soon forgotten as life ground onward in Kakuma Refugee Camp.

Many months later, near Christmas of 1995, Michel heard his name announced on the public address system. He was being summoned to the central compound. A man named James Lynch wanted to see him.

Lynch was an American resettlement officer who worked with the United Nations. His official title was durable solutions officer, a moniker Michel found rather amusing.

Lynch came to the camp once a year to interview selected refugees and determine which durable solution might suit them. Was it safe for the person to go back to his home country? Should he become integrated as a Kenyan citizen or should he be sent to another country altogether, perhaps in Europe, Australia or North America?

Michel knew Lynch to be a man of influence and he was well aware that only a privileged few were given the opportunity to state their case before the durable solutions officer each year. The officer's annual appearance always reminded Michel of someone holding a single loaf of bread above a starving crowd where everyone is waving their hands and shouting, "Pick me! Pick me! Pick me!"

He was amazed, therefore, to hear Lynch announcing over the public address system, "I wish to speak with Michel Lwamba."

Michel wondered how this man even knew his name and why he was being singled out of this multitude of thousands.

His mind immediately sped backward. The university students he had spoken with—were they spies? Had they used the information he provided against him?

Fear squeezed his heart.

"Oh God," he prayed in desperation, "is it happening to me all over again? I thought I had forgiven everything and put it behind me. Was I wrong? Is it back in my face again?"

Twice Michel's name was called with instructions to come to the central compound. The first time he ignored it. The second time, something within him said, "Why not go and talk to this man?"

A vehicle was sent to the Zairean community to pick him up. It had been a long time since Michel rode in a motorized vehicle, especially a big one with aerials bristling out all over it.

The people in the Zairean community were very anxious at the sight of Michel being escorted into the official-looking limousine. "Why is he being arrested?" they inquired. "Michel has done nothing wrong. He is a good person."

Michel was experiencing his own set of emotions as the big car neared the central compound. "I am in God's hands," he told himself firmly. "If this is my day, then it is my day."

The compound gates opened.

The car rolled through and the gates closed behind it.

Michel was escorted to the durable solutions officer. James Lynch introduced himself. On his desk was a sheet of paper bearing a list of names. Michel saw his own name, written in large letters, at the top of the list.

Lynch shook Michel's hand and invited him to sit down.

Michel sat, uncomfortably aware of his shabby appearance. He was painfully thin and wearing torn-off jeans and a pair of old sandals given to him by a friend. Like most of the refugees, his hair was cut close to the scalp, the only sensible way to keep it, given the wind and dirt that constantly blew through the camp.

"I have something to give you for Christmas," Lynch informed him pleasantly.

"And what is that?"

"I have heard your story. I know you have a family and that you have a reputation in the refugee community for being a peacemaker. It is my opinion that you have been in this camp long enough."

He went on. "You can't go back to Zaire and you can't stay in Kenya because this country is already overcrowded. The only durable solution I can find for you is to send you to another country where you can pursue further education."

Michel was stunned. Was Lynch really serious? Or was he just trying to trick him into going back to Nairobi so he could be captured and deported to Zaire?

Lynch reached into his pocket and pulled out a package of forms. He gave one to Michel and instructed him to fill it out.

"I also want you to give me the names of five other families in this camp who you think deserve the same opportunity," Lynch said, pulling out several more sheets. "Here are the forms for them."

"This can't be true," Michel told himself. "Surely I'm dreaming."

"Or," he wondered, "is this God's hand at work?"

Michel began filling out the form for his little family. Remembering his vow to live in Canada someday, he put that country down as his destination of choice.

"It's not safe for me to stay overnight in the camp," Lynch told Michel, "so I am returning to Nairobi this afternoon. But I'll be back tomorrow with a camera. I'll need to take a picture of you, your brother, your sister and your daughter."

Again, Michel was suspicious. Why did Lynch want pictures and what did he plan to do with them? Was the Zairean government using Lynch the way they had used others? Maybe it was a trick and they would all end up dead.

Another voice said, "If it's going to happen, let it happen."

The next day, Lynch returned with his camera. The pictures, he assured Michel, were for identification purposes.

He took photographs of Michel and the girls, but when it was Aliston's turn, he was nowhere to be found.

Michel knew his younger brother had gone to the hospital for malaria treatment, so he headed there to look for him.

As he searched, he was careful not to mention why he needed Aliston. Lynch had warned him not to speak about the possibility of leaving the camp because it would only stir up jealousy.

Michel could appreciate the wisdom of that. There were many who had been in the camp much longer than him and his family. Naturally, these people would feel that they should be first in line to receive such an opportunity. He could well imagine the arguments. "You are the leader," some would say. "You should be the last one to leave."

The secrecy imposed other problems, too. How could he possibly recommend five other families for immigration to Canada and not tell them? It was difficult to keep something as life changing as this a secret.

But he refused to dwell on the negatives and concentrated, instead, on looking for his brother.

Aliston was nowhere to be found.

"Write your brother's name on the form," Lynch told him, "but when I come again with the resettlement agent from the Canadian High Commission, we will need to see your brother and take his photograph so he can be identified."

At 2:00, Lynch left. At 3:00, Aliston showed up. He could hardly believe the news his brother had to tell him.

Now Michel was faced with the task of choosing five other families who would have the opportunity to trade the refugee camp for a new life of freedom and opportunity.

In the end, he selected families with children.

"I chose people with small children because, to me, the little ones are the angels," Michel explains. "They were born in the camp and don't know anything else. They are suffering for no reason of their own. That doesn't mean there weren't plenty of single people who deserved to be rescued, but it seemed to me that these little kids deserved a chance to grow up and do something good with their lives."

As he presented the list to Lynch, he was struck by the similarity between his actions and the biblical account of the angel who appeared from time to time at the pool of Bethesda to move the water. Whoever happened to get into the water first was healed. Here, too, only a few would find relief from their suffering.

About two months later, a Canadian immigration officer arrived at Kakuma to speak with the Lwambas and the five new applicant families. Michel was required to repeat how he and his little family had come to be in the refugee camp and why they couldn't go back to their own country.

There were some tense moments when the resettlement officer met Aliston. "You say this is your younger brother?" he challenged Michel. "He can't be. He's bigger than you are."

Michel explained that although Aliston was younger, he was indeed bigger in size. "I told him I had lost a lot of weight from the constant worry of how to keep my family alive."

When the interview was over and the paperwork completed, something still nagged at Michel's mind. "Add Fabian's name to the list."

"There was a place on the application form to write the names of family members," he says. "It didn't matter whether you thought they were alive or dead, you put them down anyway. The idea was if someone with your family name ever came to the United Nations, their name would be cross-checked with the files and if it appeared on a family list, the person was automatically eligible for reunification with the rest of the family."

Michel declared everyone in his immediate family, including Betty and Fabian.

When the list was complete, the resettlement officer took a pen and underlined the list with a final, bold stroke. That was it. No more names could be added.

Through the whole process, Michel had sensed the powers of darkness and evil trying to slam shut this unexpected door to hope and freedom. At one point, when the forms were completed and he was putting them in the officer's hands, a scorching gust of wind knifed through the enclosure, snatching the papers from the officer's hand and scattering them in all directions.

The officer was taken by surprise; Michel wasn't.

"I knew Satan was jealous because of what God was doing for us," he says. "It made me angry that this would happen. I said, 'In the name of Jesus....' and we ran outside to gather up all the papers. They were dirty and covered with dust, but everything was there."

The next step for the four Lwambas was to go to Nairobi for medical check-ups. It meant a few days in the city, then back to the camp to wait for their travel arrangements to be made.

Michel could have stayed on in Nairobi, but he chose to return to Kakuma with Aliston and the girls. He wanted them all to be together, particularly now that the Zairean community knew they were leaving. As Lynch had predicted, many felt betrayed and had begun treating the Lwambas like enemies.

In March of 1996, Michel, Aliston, Gisele and Sakina Lwamba left Kakuma Refugee Camp for good. They had lived there for five long years. Sakina was only two when the four escaped from Lubumbashi; now she was seven.

They would wait in Nairobi until the immigration process and their travel arrangements were complete. Michel was warned it could take up to 12 weeks. The Government of Canada had more checking to do to make sure there was no criminal activity in his background. And there were more medical screening tests to be done for diseases like tuberculosis, HIV/AIDS and syphilis. As well, the High Commission had to reassess their situation and decide which part of Canada would be the safest for them.

It was decided that the prairie province of Saskatchewan would be a good choice. In the quiet city of Saskatoon there seemed little likelihood of Michel encountering Zaireans who might be a threat to him. He was told the prairie city need not be his final destination, but that it would serve him well as a first.

In the meantime, Michel, Aliston and the girls had to bide their time. Fortunately, Durable Solutions Officer James Lynch offered Michel part-time work as a translator for incoming refugees from Zaire.

Michel accepted the position with one condition. "You know my situation," he told Lynch. "As we say in Zaire, 'Someone who has been bitten by a snake is often afraid of an ordinary rope.' Some of these people could easily be relatives of the people I persuaded to demonstrate with me in Lubumbashi. They might wish me harm and after five years in a refugee camp, I have no desire to go back there or to have someone gun me down in front of you. Could you please arrange it so I can have a look at the candidates before I come in to interpret for them?"

Lynch agreed and in each case the applicants were first seated in a library so Michel could pass by unobtrusively and determine whether or not it was safe for him to interact face to face with them.

As the Zairean candidates told their stories in French, Michel repeated them in English so James Lynch could document the accounts. Lynch had the authority to accept or reject the applications; sadly, many were rejected. Some were turned down because of the new United Nations regulation that said asylum had to be sought in the first country the person entered after leaving their own. The only exception was if the applicant could come up with good reasons why being returned to that country would be unsafe for them.

"Lots of times while I worked as an interpreter for James Lynch, I cried," Michel recalls. "Someone would come and explain their problem to me and I would translate what they said. But sometimes James Lynch said, 'No, I can't take this case.' Then the person would come back to me and beg me to help. It was very hard to bear that burden because I knew the person was telling the truth. Some of these people had been sleeping outside for a month without any food. I knew they would die right there outside the United Nations compound, but I couldn't do anything to help them, even though I knew they were just like me, carrying a very heavy load. Sometimes they blamed me for not doing anything. They thought I had influence, but I didn't. I was just a go-between."

Having the job with the United Nations meant Michel could afford to rent a tiny one-room apartment for his family. There, Aliston, now 18, 12-year-old Gisele and 7-year-old Sakina stayed in relative safety, waiting each day for Michel to come home from work.

But despite the security of the apartment's four walls, Michel still lived in fear. He knew the Zairean government had not stopped looking for him; the fact that the Zairean embassy was very close to where they lived only increased his anxiety and sense of vulnerability.

He always made sure the door was securely locked at night and prayed for God's protection so that he might wake up in the morning with his family. Even so, the merest sound outside the door or the lightest tap would keep him awake for hours.

Occasionally, James Lynch stopped by to make sure the Lwambas were all right. Lynch was the only one who knew their whereabouts. Michel didn't trust anyone else. They were so close to leaving the country and he didn't want anything to jeopardize their departure.

Rumours about President Mobutu's declining health gave no measure of comfort because Michel knew Mobutu was more of a system than merely a person. His influence had spread throughout all of east-central Africa through his relationships and liaisons with other governments. It was said that his people knew where every Zairean refugee was and even what they talked about.

Michel had also heard that there was still a price on his head and that as the president of the student political party, he was being named as the person responsible for all the killings in Lubumbashi. Understandably, he feared the parents of the young people killed might be persuaded to turn him in for the reward money.

At one point, he became so fearful that he said to James Lynch, "Instead of giving me a job, why don't you send me back to the refugee camp and just come and pick me up when it's time to leave the country?"

Lynch reminded him that he was safe under the United Nations' protection, but Michel's trust was limited. What could the UN do, he asked himself, if the Zairean government decided to seize him? They wouldn't inform the United Nations until it was all over and he was back in Zaire—or dead.

But in the midst of all of this, there were encouraging things happening, too. The preliminary medical tests all came back clean, something that Michel counted as a blessing. He knew of immigration applicants who were required to go back several times for repeat checkups. He continued to be amazed that in all the time they were at the camp, none of them contracted any of the diseases that would prevent them from immigrating to Canada.

Gisele still suffered from her sickle cell disorder, which was a worry. Michel had decided that if the condition made her ineligible for immigration, he would not go either. He would never leave Gisele behind, even if it meant cancelling their application and waiting for the obligatory five years to apply again.

The time for departure drew nearer and nearer, but Michel didn't allow himself to look ahead. He knew he wouldn't feel safe until the plane had lifted off the runway in Nairobi and was on its way to Canada. Through the International Organization of World Immigration, he had heard of more than one case where refugees disappeared from the Kenyan airport just as they were about to board their flight out of the country.

A curious incident happened shortly before their scheduled departure that sent a fresh wave of fear coursing through Michel's veins. An acquaintance—a fellow Zairean—approached him one day and announced, "We know you are going to Canada. Would you mind leaving us your stuff?"

Michel was shocked and quite distressed. How did this person know he was travelling and especially, his destination? And who exactly was "we"? Even more alarming, how did they know his exact departure date? The possibilities took him to a new level of anxiety.

And then there was another complication.

Michel didn't often have the opportunity to attend church in Nairobi. With the constant influx of refugees pouring into the city, he generally worked seven days a week. But one Sunday, about three months before they were to leave, he had the morning free and decided to go to church.

There were two churches near the apartment. Michel had visited both, but found the worship style of the furthest one to be more appealing to him. On this particular day, he was headed for the closer church. In fact, he was just about to enter its door when his heart was filled with a strong desire to go to the other one.

The church was large and had a congregation of about 800 people. Michel slid into a seat near the back and tried his best to enter into the worship.

"I was listening," he recalls, "but my spirit was uneasy. My concentration kept drifting in and out. I had the feeling something was about to happen."

When the pastor finished preaching, he issued an invitation for people in need of repentance or prayer to come to the front. From the opposite side at the back of the church, Michel saw a woman move forward. His heart leaped in his chest and began to race wildly. He could see only the back of the woman's head, but there was something hauntingly familiar about her.

He strained to get a better look, but there were too many people moving forward and he lost sight of her.

The pastor said, "Let us pray."

Michel closed his eyes, but his mind was not on the prayer. Could this woman be Betty—his wife? She certainly looked like Betty, at least from the back. Mind you, it had been five long years—five years in which he had accepted that his wife was most likely dead. He had never considered that she might still be alive and of all things, living here in Nairobi.

By the time the pastor said "Amen" and people began returning to their seats, Michel had made it to the other side of the church. He watched the woman coming up the aisle.

It certainly looked like Betty.

Then she looked up.

It was her, in the middle of the aisle, in the midst of the congregation, the two threw their arms around each other, hugging and weeping for joy.

They exclaimed over and over again about this amazing miracle of God that was happening. Both had lived for five long years convinced the other was dead. It didn't seem possible they were together again.

The ensuing years had been very difficult for Betty, too. On the day of the demonstration, she and her newborn baby boy Rodrigue were away from the compound visiting relatives. When the military came to the house searching for Michel, they seized Betty and put her in prison in his place. According to Zairean law, when a husband has broken the law and cannot be found, his wife is imprisoned on his behalf until he is located.

"Talk to your relatives," the authorities ordered Betty. "Tell them to search for your husband. When he comes, we will let you go."

Of course, Michel did not show up and Betty and the baby remained in jail. It was a brutal and dangerous place. Like every other government institution, the prison system in Zaire was rampant with corruption, despite the fact that a good portion of the inmates were people whose only crime was disagreeing with the government. Many died of torture and beatings without ever going to trial.

That same corruption worked in Betty's favour.

Nuns from the local Catholic parish conducted a ministry of bringing food and other necessities to prisoners in jail. These women came from the same church whose priest helped Michel and the others escape. The nuns were aware of Betty's precarious situation and devised a way for her to escape.

Eight months after her arrest, the sisters bribed the guards and smuggled Betty and the baby out of prison.

The safest thing seemed to be for Betty to go to Kenya. So, dressed in a nun's habit, Betty was driven out of Lubumbashi in the guise of a Catholic sister delivering an abandoned child to an orphanage in Nairobi.

Once there, the nuns found temporary shelter for Betty in the home of a pastor where she and Rodrigue were allowed to stay while she looked for Michel. Of course, she didn't find him and in the five years since, her place of residence had changed several times.

Now, by a miracle of God, she and Michel were together again.

Betty and Rodrigue immediately went to live with Michel, Aliston, Gisele and Sakina in the apartment, but the reunion was bittersweet. Michel had a dilemma. Now he didn't know if he wanted to leave Africa. It would mean leaving Betty and their young son behind again and he didn't know if he could do that.

He took Betty to the immigration people to see if she and Rodrigue could be added to his visa, but the answer was a flat "No." Betty had never spent any time in a refugee camp and therefore did not qualify as a conventional registered refugee.

There were two options; neither was satisfactory. Michel could continue with the arrangements to go to Canada and try to sponsor Betty and Rodrigue once he got there, or he could stay in Nairobi with Betty and start the whole immigration process over again for the whole family. It would mean waiting five years before they applied again.

"It was a very difficult decision," Michel says. "We were all leaving and she was staying behind. My heart was broken all over again. At the airport, I waved goodbye to my wife, not knowing if I would ever see her again."

It was a time of uncertainty on all fronts. The Lwambas were leaving Africa permanently, heading for an unfamiliar place, not knowing who they would meet or what sorts of situations they were going to encounter. Worse, they were leaving without knowing for certain what had happened to the rest of their family. Finding Betty was a miracle beyond anything Michel had ever imagined, but was it possible that others in the family had survived, too? It seemed unlikely.

Michel thought about his brother Fabian a great deal. His head said Fabian was dead, but his heart stubbornly refused to accept it. He clung to the memory of two vivid dreams he'd had in the camp about being with Fabian again. In his dreams, the two of them were singing together. Friends said it was because he was thinking too much about his brother.

In November of 1996, the Lwambas finally left Africa for Canada. They landed in Saskatoon amidst a full-blown Canadian winter. The weather was unseasonably cold, even for Saskatchewan. The temperature, in the −30s, was a nasty shock to their systems.

The first time Michel saw his breath, he was gravely concerned. How could it be, he wondered, that smoke was coming out of his mouth when he wasn't smoking a cigarette? His first thought was that he had developed a serious lung problem.

The four were put up in a hotel for two weeks until suitable housing arrangements could be made.

The only people they met those first few days were representatives from Immigration Canada and a Cambodian man by the name of Sarath Hem who worked for the Open Door Society, a local organization dedicated to helping new immigrants get settled and integrated into Canadian society.

Through Sarath Hem and the Open Door Society, the Lwambas were able to acquire a furnished apartment and make arrangements for the two girls to start school. Michel and Aliston attended orientation classes and English lessons.

Coming to terms with the fact that they now lived in a free and democratic society where one need not be suspicious of every stranger and there was no cause to constantly look over one's shoulder, was difficult. Some time after arriving in Saskatoon, Michel had a heart-stopping experience that made him realize just how close to the surface his fears and insecurities still were.

He was riding a bicycle near his apartment building when suddenly, a car driven by a young man trying to evade police lost control and lurched over the curb and onto the sidewalk, very nearly hitting the bicycle. Already stunned by the close call, Michel suddenly found himself surrounded by uniformed policemen with weapons drawn. He was petrified. His mind raced through all sorts of desperate scenarios, even as he watched the officers seize and arrest the culprit. The incident brought back a flood of painful and fear-filled memories from home. Michel had no way of knowing this type of occurrence was not the norm in a place like Saskatoon.

Living among strangers in a strange new culture was a very lonely experience for Michel. The days were long and he filled them with looking after his family and writing letters to his friends back in Kakuma Refugee Camp.

He wrote about 20 letters in all and sent them to the United Nations man, Mr. Macomfrey, to be delivered to Michel's friends. He wanted them to know where he was and how things were going. One letter he sent was to his friend Aruga.

Weeks passed.

One morning Michel went downstairs to clean out his mailbox, which was always overflowing with advertising circulars or mail for the previous tenant. On this particular morning, there was a letter addressed to him. It was from Kakuma Refugee Camp.

His eyes brightened. It would be good to hear from one of his friends in the camp.

He ran upstairs and quickly tore open the envelope.

As he scanned the enclosed page, his legs crumpled beneath him.

The letter was from Fabian.

AFRICA

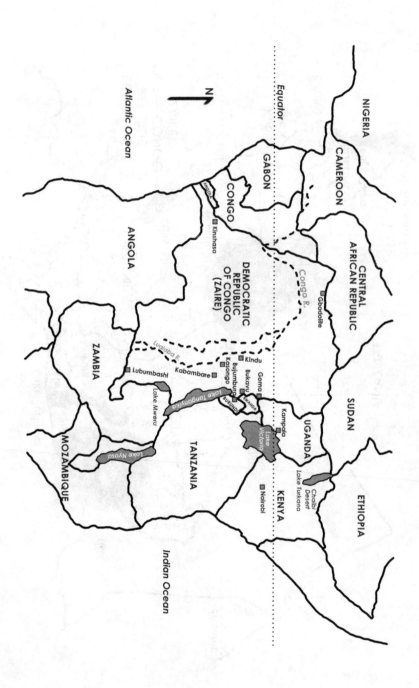

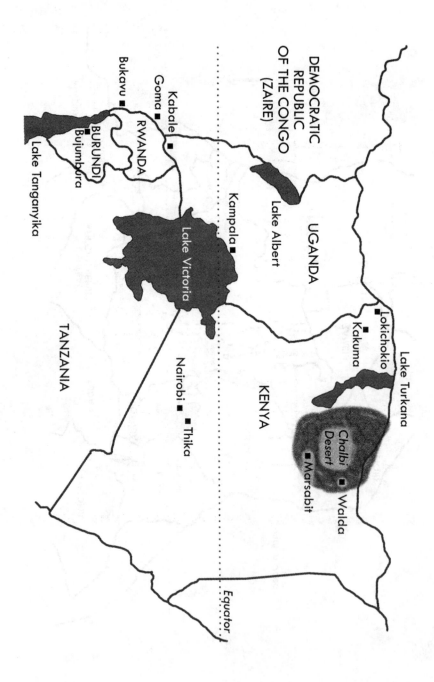

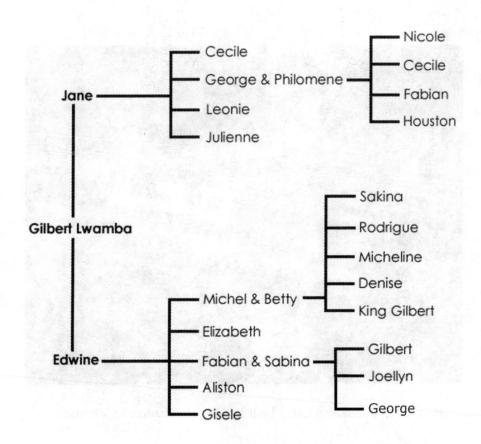

Family Tree of Gilbert Lwamba

Church in Kukama Camp built by Michel, Aliston and a friend

Fence marking the food distribution, head count and assessment centre close to where the Congolese stayed

Distribution day at Kukama Camp
Background: tent poles given after three months

Hospital at Kukama Camp where Michel volunteered as a translator for
the Congolese refugees

Entrance to Kukama Camp
The sign reads "Dry Bones," the name Kukama means "dry bones"
because this was the place where the bones of the dead were left to dry
out in the sun.

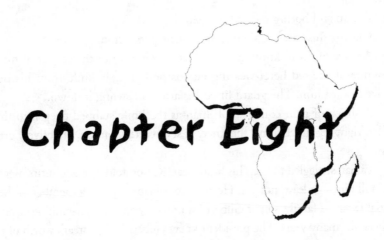

Chapter Eight

Fabian was alive, but not well.

He was living in Kakuma Refugee Camp where he had been transferred several months earlier—very near, in fact, to the time that Michel and the others left for Nairobi.

Nearly six years had passed since the student demonstration in Lubumbashi when the brothers lost sight of one another. For all of them, the years were fraught with terror, hardship and suffering.

When Mobutu's DSP forces turned their machine guns and their tear gas on the crowd of student demonstrators, Fabian was overcome by the tear gas. While struggling to regain his vision, he was seized and shoved into a military vehicle. There he was blindfolded and whisked away to a place he remembers only as being "very dark and very weird." It was where the DSP brought their victims for interrogation and torture. Going by the shouts and screams of pain coming from the nearby rooms, Fabian could tell he was not the only one to be captured.

The agents began the questioning. Where was his brother, Michel Lwamba? Where was the rest of the family likely to be?

Fabian did not answer.

The guards threw him to the floor. His head hit the concrete with a painful, bone-jarring crack that broke the skin. Blood began to ooze from the wound.

Still he refused to answer their questions.

His captors began kicking him, landing vicious blows to his head, his back and his stomach with their jackbooted feet. They ground his face into the concrete floor.

Fabian stubbornly refused to yield.

Clearly, this case required more drastic persuasion.

A wave of dread knotted Fabian's stomach. Out of the corner of his eye he saw one of the red beret-wearing guards pull an ugly knife from his belt and move toward him. The guard lifted his arm and swung it down.

A shock of pain convulsed Fabian as the knife stabbed deep into the back of his right leg just behind the knee. It severed the tendon, effectively crippling him.

Fabian struggled to keep his head clear. Reason told him Mobutu's men would not kill him—at least, not yet. He was too valuable a prize, a member of the influential Lwamba family, son of Gilbert Lwamba, a popular high-ranking government official for many years. The president knew Gilbert had a career's worth of incriminating political documents locked away safely, if not in the Lubumbashi residence, then at one of the other family holdings. If they hoped to learn anything of value from Gilbert's son, it was in their best interest to keep him alive.

If they had plans to interrogate Fabian further, the plans were put on hold by the stab wound, which was now bleeding so furiously their prisoner was in danger of bleeding to death. Reluctantly, they loaded him into a truck and transported him to the hospital for treatment.

Fabian remained in Lubumbashi Hospital for 14 days, gravely ill and in excruciating pain. Bodyguards were posted by his bed to keep him under constant surveillance until he was recovered enough to undergo more questioning.

It seemed Fabian's fate was sealed.

But behind the scenes, other events were taking place. Fabian's uncle, Mokili Awazi, his mother Edwine's brother, had heard about Fabian's arrest and his subsequent transfer to the hospital. As a lieutenant in the regular army, Mokili used his influence to have a bribe paid to the bodyguards to look the other way while Fabian was taken out of the hospital.

Fabian believes the bribe was probably a substantial one, because the bodyguards would have known full well their own lives were in jeopardy if they allowed their prisoner to escape.

Lieutenant Mokili Awazi came to the hospital to make sure the escape plan was successful, but he did not make contact. As Fabian was being hustled out of the building in a wheelchair, he saw his uncle in the distance.

Mokili lifted his hand in farewell.

It was the last time Fabian ever saw him. He would learn later that Mokili and his entire family, save one, were murdered for helping Fabian escape.

At the time of the escape, Fabian had no idea what was happening to him. He knew only that he was being wheeled out of the hospital and put in a waiting car by a stranger who warned, "Do not say a word. We're taking you out of here. You will be fine."

Fabian didn't believe a word of it. He was convinced he was on his way to die. He had seen too many of his friends disappear to believe otherwise.

The vehicle travelled through the city and out of Lubumbashi into the country. From the direction they were going, Fabian guessed they must be heading for the Ugandan border. The further they travelled, the more clearly the realization came that he had indeed been rescued and that he was being taken somewhere safe, somewhere far from the chaos in Lubumbashi.

At one point, the car stopped in Kivu, home territory for the Lwamba clan. Fabian knew the area intimately. In fact, the family had a residence there, but he knew it would be suicide to try and hide there. Besides, Mokili had already made arrangements for him to connect with a trucking company that did long distance hauling between Zaire and other parts of east Africa. The company was used by local Catholic churches to transport supplies from Nairobi, Kenya, to Zaire. It would eventually take him to Nairobi.

Travelling in the guise of a representative of the Catholic church, Fabian became the third member of a three-man hauling crew.

At the beginning, he was too sick to do anything more than just ride along. Without the proper treatment, his leg wound had become infected. It eventually healed, but it was many, many months before Fabian could walk properly again without pain.

For the first month, the truck shuttled goods from point to point within Zaire. Fabian was on edge the whole time. He knew as long as he remained in Zaire, his life was in grave danger.

His strongest instinct was to dash across the border into Burundi and hide out in one of the family residences there, but the truth was there was no safe place for him in Burundi, either. The warring Rwandan Hutus and Tutsis had already moved into Burundi and were heading for Zaire. Besides, political alliances in high places meant an enemy of Zaire was an enemy of Burundi.

In late 1991, the transport truck finally crossed the Zairean border into Uganda on its eventual way to Nairobi, but there was still a long way to go. The crew continued its schedule of transporting goods from place to place, dropping off cargo, picking up new loads. From time to time they changed vehicles, but Fabian and the crew remained constant.

Sometimes they would stop in a town for two or three days. The drivers let Fabian sleep in the truck where he was out of sight. He was grateful for their consideration and thankful he was in the company of ordinary Zaireans who proved to be kind and generous people.

There were many tense moments, especially when the crew encountered one of the many military roadblocks. Each time a soldier approached the truck brandishing a gun, Fabian had a mental picture of himself lying dead on the ground. The men would be ordered out of the truck and every time there were questions about Fabian's leg wound. How did he get it? Where? What were the circumstances?

Fabian spent nearly a year with the truckers, zigzagging across Uganda and northeastern Zaire. They passed Christmas of 1991 in the relative calm of Kampala, Uganda's capital.

It was a very difficult time for him. All around, people were gathering together. Families were preparing for Christmas. He was alone with his memories of Christmases back home. They were always such happy family times. He wondered where his mother and father were. What was going on at home? What had happened to Michel? Was he alive? Or was he dead?

During the stop in Kampala, Fabian attended a church service where he made the acquaintance of a Canadian woman named Thelma Burns.

Thelma worked in the refugee department of the Canadian embassy in Kampala. She noticed that Fabian did not look Ugandan and approached him after the service.

She asked his name.

"Fabian," he answered, purposely neglecting to add his surname.

"You are French," she observed. "Are you from Zaire?"

He nodded, hoping she wouldn't ask any more questions. He wasn't ready to reveal all that had happened to bring him from his home in Zaire to this place.

"Are you running from something?" she pressed. "Are you a refugee? Are you hoping to get to east Africa?"

"No," Fabian protested. Yes, he was running, but he didn't want to think of himself as a refugee. He had heard about refugees and couldn't bear the thought of living like one. Besides, he told himself, leaving Zaire was only temporary. As soon as everything settled down, he would head back home.

"If you were a refugee, I could help you," Thelma said. "Is there anything I can do for you right now? Do you need anything?"

"I've hurt my leg and I'm in a lot of pain," Fabian admitted.

Thelma made a trip to the pharmacy and brought back some medicines, which she gave to Fabian along with some Ugandan money. "I wish I could help you more," she said. "Good luck if you're going to east Africa."

Not many days later, the transport truck finally passed through the border point of Malaba and into Kenya.

It was very early in the morning when they reached Nairobi.

"It was a huge town," Fabian recalls. "I had never been there before, but I'd heard a lot about it. Nairobi had the reputation of being a peaceful city, a place free of war."

Even so, he knew he had to be careful.

He wanted to be as far away from the Zairean embassy as possible, but that was difficult because the United Nations building, where he needed to go, was in the same area as all the foreign embassies. He knew from conversations with other people that the Zaireans kept a close eye on everyone coming to the UN. They even had ways, it was said, of hearing what was being discussed and went to extreme lengths to silence any Zairean who dared to speak out about the government's crimes and abuses. Somehow, Mobutu had been successful in keeping what was happening in Zaire a secret from the rest of the world and he didn't want anyone speaking out. To that end, he had issued a specific directive to arrest any student who survived the university massacre and return them to Zaire for trial and prosecution.

It was a difficult parting when Fabian's truck driver friends finally dropped him off at the United Nations compound. After nearly a year of living and working together, the men had become like family to him. Now, he was losing his family all over again.

The United Nations officials were sympathetic. "We know you Zaireans have been through some awful things," they said. "All we can do is put you in a camp with the other refugees, but it will take a while."

In the meantime, Fabian was given accommodation in a cheap hotel with some other Zairean students.

The Kenyan authorities proved less sympathetic. Security people from the government paid the young Zaireans a call.

"Which one of you is Jean Paul?" they inquired. Jean Paul was a young Christian minister who had run for his life from Zaire.

"Which of you is Fabian?"

An icy chill went down Fabian's spine. How did they know his name? And what did they want with him?

"We are here to make sure you boys are not in Kenya to make trouble. Just remember, we know what you did and we can send you back to Zaire at any time. If we decide to, you can be face to face with Mobutu in a couple of hours." They gave a nasty laugh. "Who knows? Maybe you'll be seeing him for supper tonight."

One bright spot for Fabian was meeting Bakini, a young doctor who hailed from Goma in eastern Zaire. Bakini was someone Fabian instinctively knew that he could trust. He found him easy to talk to and the two quickly became friends.

But Bakini had his own set of problems. He had managed to escape with his wife, but their children and rest of the family were still back in Zaire.

The couple had spent some time in Thika, a small refugee camp near Nairobi. Thika was a model refugee camp, the one the United Nations liked to show to the rest of the world. There, hired personnel cooked for the refugees and even washed their clothes. But with the flood of refugees now pouring into the capital, Thika was too overcrowded to remain viable. It was being shut down and the residents reassigned to other camps, primarily Kakuma and Walda.

Fabian was pleased to learn that he and his new friend were assigned to the same camp. With his friend there, he told himself, life in the camp might be more tolerable.

Walda was in the north-eastern part of Kenya, a two-day journey away from Nairobi. The refugees were transferred there in United Nations buses. Bakini was assigned to a bus that left the morning before Fabian's.

The roads were poor; travel was slow. The trip necessitated spending one night on the road. Passengers had their choice of sleeping inside the bus or outside under the stars.

When Fabian's bus arrived at the overnight stopping place the next day, there was a sense of tragedy in the air that was almost palpable. He soon learned why.

No one had informed the refugees that the area through which they were passing was populated by Ethiopian rebels who made regular raids on the nearby refugee camp to steal whatever they could. When the bus carrying Fabian's doctor friend stopped the previous evening, the bandits descended upon them in the night. Bakini was shot dead where he slept.

Fabian was devastated. His grief was beyond words, especially when he saw how disrespectfully his doctor friend had been buried, under a scraped together pile of stones.

Fabian was still in shock the following day when the bus stopped at a police roadblock near the town of Marsabit. He sat in a daze while uniformed officers climbed aboard the bus and began a systematic check of all the passengers. Fabian had no idea what was happening.

Suddenly, one of the officers declared, "This is the man we're looking for."

Fabian looked up. They were pointing at him.

He was stunned.

"Get out," the officer ordered roughly. The policemen with him turned their guns on Fabian.

Bewildered and shaking with fear, Fabian got down from the bus.

By this time, the UN bus driver had gathered up enough courage to ask what was going on. "These people are refugees," he reminded the policemen.

"We know and that's exactly who we're looking for. This man is Ethiopian. He killed a policeman in Nairobi."

"But I'm not Ethiopian," Fabian protested frantically. "See—?" He hauled out the identification document or "protection letter" the United Nations had issued him. "Here are my papers. You can see for yourself I'm not from Ethiopia."

Fabian fully expected he would be shot where he stood, but after checking his papers, the authorities decided he was not the man they were looking for, after all. They let him go. He was still trembling when they reached Walda Refugee Camp several hours later.

Walda turned out to be one more in a long line of shocks.

"I don't think I'll ever find the words to describe Walda Refugee Camp," Fabian says. "Every bush and every shrub in that desert place was a thorn bush. People in the camp had to build their shelters in and around thorn bushes, so whether you were sleeping or walking, you were constantly plagued by thorns."

Walda was a relatively new refugee camp created in an area inhabited by two primitive tribes, the Garis and Baranas. Originally from Ethiopia, these tribes had migrated to this part of Kenya generations ago. Their state of abysmal poverty eventually came to the attention of the United Nations, which initiated an aid program to help the starving Garis and Baranas survive in the near-famine conditions. Since aid was already coming to the area, the UN reckoned that the current flood of refugees could be easily managed if they were camped and maintained alongside the Garis and Baranas.

This, of course, did not sit well with the tribespeople. Though they constantly waged war between themselves, they were united in the knowledge that they did not want outsiders in their territory. From the very outset, they began a campaign of abuse, harassment and overt violence against the intruders.

As Fabian's group entered the refugee camp, the first thing to greet them was the incredible stench of decaying cattle carcasses that littered the landscape. The cattle belonged to the Barana people, who depended on the rains for water. When it rained, the cows grew big and fat; when it was dry, they died and their carcasses were left to rot where they fell.

The camp itself was a shanty city of thousands upon thousands of very old, very small, yellow tents. The tents were issued one to a family and even though they were intended to accommodate only one person, four were expected to squeeze inside.

The tent fabric was so thin that the shaky shelter seemed in constant danger of blowing away in the fierce winds that came off the distant Indian Ocean at night. The winds were suffocatingly hot and heavy with moisture. Their roar made sleeping nearly impossible.

Like Michel's Kakuma Camp, Walda had its distinctive ethnic communities. Fabian was assigned to the Zairean sector, where he tried in vain to find a vacant spot among the thorn bushes to pitch his tent. He and the three other young men who would share the quarters dug a hollow in the ground and set the tent over top. Their strategy was twofold. Not only would it be cooler, but the recess in the ground would be a place to hide when gunfire erupted within the camp—as it always did, at least three or four times a week.

Of course, there was no electricity in Walda and Fabian had never experienced such darkness. From July to November the nights were so densely black, one could see no further than about three metres ahead. Making things dramatically more dangerous were the whizzing bullets that filled the night air on a regular basis.

"Walda was a horrible place to be," Fabian says. "There were problems and violence everywhere, even within the Zairean community. We didn't trust each other. You didn't dare trust the person next to you. You didn't dare tell him your last name because you didn't know who he was. Someone would show you a picture and you realized he used to be one of Mobutu's bodyguards. Another would say, 'I was in Israel getting military training.' You know he was probably one of Mobutu's DSP, maybe even someone involved in the student massacre. You just didn't know who you could trust."

The Zaireans were positioned between the Ethiopian and Sudanese communities, both of which were heavily armed. The Sudanese were from Christian and animist tribes in southern Sudan and constantly faced the possibility of a raid from their well-armed northern Sudanese Muslim enemies. They considered Walda to be their military base. Here they lived, married and produced as many children as possible to provide future fighters for the ongoing civil war in their country.

On the other side were the Ethiopians, also heavily armed.

There was always shooting and killing going on in Walda. Sometimes it got so bad that the UN staff who ran the camp escaped to Nairobi for a few days until things settled down. That left more than 200,000 people in a state of anarchy. Whoever survived, survived. If someone was shot or wounded, there was no one at the camp hospital to treat them.

Conditions in the camp were abysmal. The camp was plagued with flies and insects. "Every morning when you got up, your body was covered with flies looking for a way to get inside," Fabian says. "You tried to keep yourself covered, but anywhere you were exposed, they were there."

Compounding the insect problem was the absence of latrines. Refugees were instructed to dig a hole in the sand and cover it up afterward, but most didn't bother and simply used the bushes around the camp as their toilet. The constant winds blew the foul stench of exposed human excrement into the camp, where it permeated everything, including the food.

Water was in very short supply in Walda. Residents collected as much of the natural rainfall as they could, but that water was used only for drinking and cooking. Nothing was wasted on personal hygiene.

Sickness was rampant. The little infirmary run by Médecins Sans Frontières was always filled to overflowing. Fabian got a first-hand look at conditions when a friend came down with typhoid fever and Fabian volunteered to take a turn at the hospital to look after him during the night.

What he saw stunned him. The place was jam-packed with sick people. Every bed had two occupants and as soon as one patient showed the slightest sign of improvement, he was discharged so an even sicker person could get treatment. Epidemics spread like wildfire. By the second day in hospital, a patient was guaranteed to have contracted whatever was going around. Malaria was as common as the flu.

Some patients didn't even get a bed. Those with diarrhea slept on the ground outside the hospital where they became prey to even deadlier dangers like snakes and scorpions.

Fabian had his own run-in with a scorpion. "They were everywhere," he says, "even under your bed. You had to be so careful. I was in my tent when a scorpion bit me on my middle finger. The poison paralyzed my arm as it moved toward my chest. My heart started to burn and I almost lost consciousness. My friends rushed me over to a refugee who had been a medical student in Zaire and now worked in the camp with Médecins Sans Frontières. He had some medicine with him and gave me an injection. I survived, but it was a week before I could do anything. The pain of that little bite was incredible. I'd never experienced anything like it."

Another danger was the wild animals that crept into the camp on a regular basis. Young children and the weak were vulnerable prey, as was the Sudanese community on the camp's perimeter. One woman walking with her baby on her back was attacked by vultures that pecked out the baby's eyes.

The heat was almost unbearable. The daytime temperature held at a constant 42° Celsius. Many days, Fabian couldn't think of any good reason to get up, but he did anyway, just because of the heat. Often, he rose before 5:00 in the morning. "If you waited until 8:00," he says, "the temperature inside the tent was up to 38° Celsius."

Food was distributed once every two weeks by Care International. Rations were two cups of dried beans, a quarter cup of sugar, two teaspoons of salt and some rice and oil.

Fabian learned to stretch his rations, but the biggest challenge was finding wood to make a fire to boil the beans and rice. By now his leg had healed to the point where he could hobble around a bit, but the long treks into the desert in search of firewood were excruciating. Carrying the wood back to camp on his head was a new experience. He had never carried anything on his head before and doing so gave him severe headaches.

But despite his own discomfort, a greater pain for Fabian was watching the children in the camp. They looked like the starving tots he used to see at home on television—all emaciated and pathetic looking. They were especially at risk on food Distribution Day when everyone had to stand in line and wait. Often, violence would break out because there was always someone who wanted to get to the front of the line. Fabian and some of the other young men made it a point to carry the little ones so they wouldn't get hurt.

It seemed that every day had its own fresh potential for conflict and violence. The daily quest for water could be a battlefield. Full-scale fights broke out over who should take water first, even though some might have arisen at 3:00

a.m. so they would be first. It was not uncommon for an individual to pull a knife and attack another person over it.

There was no provision for keeping order in the camp or protecting individual rights. A stabbing victim, if he were lucky, might be heaved into a wheelbarrow (the community's ambulance) and taken to the infirmary for treatment, but that only happened if there were others around who cared enough about the injured person to get involved.

"In a refugee camp, every problem is monumental," Fabian says. "It might be something as simple as someone sitting in a shadow. Another will say, 'I was sitting in that shadow first; you took my place when I got up.'"

But it was not the physical dangers that Fabian found the hardest to bear. It was the loneliness. Though he was surrounded by thousands and thousands of people, the ones who mattered in his life were gone: Michel, his parents, Aliston and George. From the stories and information that came into camp via each new refugee from Zaire, he had concluded that his family members were probably all dead. In his heart, he had accepted that he, too, would die—most likely right here in Walda Camp. And given the violence that went on continuously, his death could take place at any time.

In fact, one night the fighting and killing got so bad that Fabian could endure it no longer. He decided to run away. There was nowhere to go, of course, but he figured if he ran toward the bush, someone would probably shoot him and that would be the end of it. He would make sure his protection letter was on his person so when they came to bury his body, they would at least know who he was.

Having made up his mind, he got dressed in the darkness and gathered up his documents while tears streamed down his face.

"God, if you are there," he murmured through his tears, "I may be seeing you very soon because I'm going to make a run for it. I can't stay here any longer. If I survive, fine. If I don't, well...what's the difference? I just can't see anything here to live for."

He drew a deep breath and prepared himself.

But in that precise moment, he realized that everything outside had gone curiously still. The shooting and violence had subsided. The unexpected quiet prompted him re-evaluate his plan to end his life. "Maybe I won't run," he said to himself. "Maybe I can endure here a little longer."

Looking back today, Fabian shakes his head. "I don't understand how any of us in that camp survived," he says. "It was like being in prison. You weren't technically a prisoner, but if you decided to leave, you could never make it to Nairobi without help."

Besides that, Kenyan law required refugees to stay in the refugee camp. Anyone being sent to Nairobi for medical treatment carried a written pass stating how many days they could stay in the city and their reason for being there. If the person tried to stay longer, he would be arrested and sent back to the camp—or to his home country.

Shortly after the incident, Fabian met Adrian, a Ugandan Christian.

Adrian had somehow acquired a simple drum and had begun beating out rhythms on the drum and singing spiritual songs. As he continued day after day, people gathered around and one by one, joined in the singing. Soon Adrian was reading aloud from the Bible and praying. It wasn't long before the gatherings became full-blown praise and prayer meetings.

Fabian was one of the people who joined Adrian in singing. He was amazed at how powerful a tool music could be for encouraging people who saw no way out of their hopeless existence.

On more than one occasion, someone would come to him and say, "If you hadn't sung last night, I would have killed myself. I was going to do it, but as I listened to the song you were singing, I decided I could face another morning."

The Christian Ethiopians in camp had constructed a rough church building in their community. It was a simple mud brick structure covered with plastic, but it gave them a modicum of shelter when they gathered on Sunday mornings to worship. No one outside the Ethiopian community attended because they couldn't understand the language, but the Ethiopians agreed to let Adrian and his group use the building on Sunday afternoons. Soon, a weekly worship schedule was established with singing and prayer on Wednesday and Friday and worship and teaching on Sunday.

As in Kakuma, it wasn't only refugees who attended the services. United Nations personnel came, as well, to hear the music and listen to Adrian preaching from the Bible. The lives of many people were transformed as a result, including Fabian's.

He had never paid much attention to religion before. In the Catholic schools he attended as a child he had learned about religion, but now he was hearing about Jesus Christ and how He forgave sin and promised hope and eternal life to anyone who believed in Him.

In Walda, Fabian came to know how much God loved him. He realized that all the tangible things of the world—those material things that had been wiped out of his life—amounted to nothing. One way or another, they would all disappear anyway. But it was a tremendous comfort to learn that there was more to life than what he could see at the moment. With Jesus, he had hope for tomorrow, whether it was in heaven for eternity or for a while longer in the camp.

Fabian's happiest moments became the ones he spent in prayer. He felt close to God when he was praying and knew with a certainty that Jesus Christ was alive and living within him. The reality gave him a reason to persevere and keep standing firm.

One of the Bible lessons with which he and the others in the Walda congregation identified was the account of Jesus going into the desert to commune with His Father.

"Jesus fasted for 40 days," Fabian points out. "We could all identify with that. We knew how tough it was to be in the hot desert without food or water. We, at least, had a little sugar and bread. We said if Jesus went through that and worse, we can, too."

The congregation pastored by Adrian kept on growing and eventually constructed a simple church building of its own where they could meet for prayer, worship and Bible teaching.

As the months went by, Fabian's faith and trust in God deepened, but all around him the violence in Walda continued. It became so bad that there was talk the camp would be closed. The refugees had no idea what would become of them.

Chapter Nine

In May of 1996, about seven months before the closure and five years after he arrived at the camp, Fabian was summoned to the central compound. There, to his amazement, was his 11-year-old cousin Edwine, the daughter of his Uncle Mokili.

Edwine was in deep trauma. She had witnessed the massacre of her entire family and was the only one of them left alive. She hadn't spoken a word since the tragedy.

She was here at Walda because someone in Lubumbashi had heard there might be Lwambas in Nairobi. Edwine was taken to the UN office there, in the hope that she could be connected with her relatives. An officer, who worked in Walda Camp and knew Fabian, just happened to be in the United Nations office the day Edwine was brought in. He was on his way back to Walda and offered to take Edwine to her relative.

The moment Edwine saw Fabian, she burst into tears. He knew in that moment that no matter what happened, he had to survive—if only for Edwine's sake. He would never be free of the realization that her father—indeed her whole family—died so that he could live.

Fabian left the friends with whom he had shared a tent for the past several years and set up a new shelter for himself and his grieving cousin. Though she would not speak of the horrors she had witnessed to anyone else, she did reveal little bits of it to Fabian.

"It was very difficult for Edwine," he says. "There was so much she wanted to tell me, but she couldn't. It was too horrible. She didn't want to remember."

The camp administration wanted to interview Edwine, but she refused to go to the office. She trusted no one.

It was Edwine who brought the sad and definitive news that Fabian's parents, Gilbert and Edwine, were dead—taken away when the authorities came to the Lwamba home looking for Fabian and Michel—and never seen again. It was a devastating blow.

"When you think about all this and see what was going on all around us in the camp, it is hard to imagine that anyone could still praise God," he says, "but I did. Our family was killed, our property was plundered by soldiers, our houses were confiscated—how could I say, 'Praise God!'? But I could, because I believed God was there, watching over us."

Not long after Edwine's arrival, Walda Refugee Camp closed. The residents were told they would be transferred to other camps. The Zairean community was split in two with one half going to a camp near Mombasa, the other half going to Kakuma.

Fabian and Edwine were assigned to Kakuma.

Adrian and his fellow Ugandans were transferred to a different camp where they were placed next to a community of Muslims. The man who had pastored the Christian community in Walda so faithfully was targeted by the Muslims because he was a Christian who boldly preached about Jesus and was soon killed by poisoning.

In late December of 1996, Fabian and Edwine were loaded onto a United Nations bus for the journey to Kakuma Camp in northwest Kenya. It took three days to complete the journey over pothole-riddled roads.

With each kilometre, it became more and more evident that they were being taken to a very different part of the country from the one where they had been. For all its thorns, Walda was a relatively green place. Kakuma, it seemed, was in the middle of genuine desert.

They arrived at Kakuma in early January, 1997. Fabian's first thought was, "Surely they can't mean to leave us here."

He and Edwine were given a temporary tent and instructions to set it up in the central compound until everyone was processed and registered. It was three weeks before they were brought to the Zairean sector, where they erected their tent and unpacked their meager belongings.

Being in a new camp required adjustment. Oddly enough, life in Walda had been secure—predictable, at least.

"You woke up in the same tent every morning. You went through the same routine. You mingled with faces that, over five years, had become familiar."

In Walda, Fabian knew what to expect. In Kakuma, he didn't. He was surrounded by strangers and none were stranger than the naked Turkana people.

By now, Kakuma had become a settlement in its own right. Bisected by a dirt "street" that ran north to the Sudanese border, it was far more structured than Walda had ever been. Some members of the Ethiopian community had been in the camp so long they had established trading businesses for themselves. Their shops were enclosures made of vertical poles stuck in the ground and covered with a tent. Through the poles, one could see the shopkeeper inside.

Merchandise came from a Turkana town about five kilometres from the camp. The Ethiopian merchants bought the goods from the Turkanas and sold them to refugees in the camp at a higher price.

If a customer didn't have the money, he could trade other commodities. Fabian learned that he could trade a coke bottlecap of sugar for a basket of charcoal, which he needed to cook his bean and rice rations.

As time went on, Fabian got to know some of his fellow refugees. Most of them were students. Every one, it seemed, had a tragic story.

One young man, Robert, was from Rwanda. He escaped the infamous Hutu/Tutsi bloodbath, in which more than half a million people were killed in a couple of weeks. Robert ran for his life and was able to reach Nairobi via Uganda. He saw people massacred along the way: a six-month-old baby smashed against a tree trunk like a hunk of wood to save a bullet; people's throats slashed seconds after being told to pray to God because they would soon be dead.

While his heart ached for Robert, Fabian felt most sorry for the students whom the United Nations refused to recognize and shelter as refugees. They were known as The Refused.

The Refused were told they didn't qualify as Kenyan refugees because of the new United Nations policy that said a person must seek refugee status in the first country they entered. That meant someone from Zaire who came to Kenya via Uganda, as Fabian did before the regulation was in place, would be required to return to Uganda and seek refugee status there.

Fabian found the policy inhumane. It was common knowledge that there was no sanctuary for Zaireans in Uganda.

"For me to have reached Kenya alive was a miracle," one young man told him. "I made it through the jungle. I survived lions and rebel armies, but the friends I was with didn't. To follow that same road back would mean certain death for me."

Another said, "Out of the six of us who started out, I am the only one alive. My friends were all killed on the way to Kenya by rebels. Now the United Nations says I have to go back that same road? I cannot do it. You might as well kill me right here."

But camp officials stood firm. "If you stay here, there won't be any rations for you and if you get sick, no one will look after you."

With no rations, The Refused were prime targets for the agents who came in the name of the Red Cross soliciting blood. For every pint of blood donated, a person could get a bottle of Coke, a glass of milk or a piece of bread, a kilogram of sugar or a T-shirt. It was all for a good cause, they were told: to help Sudanese soldiers wounded in their country's ongoing civil war.

Many of The Refused gave blood repeatedly just so they could eat. One woman, desperate for milk for her children, gave so much blood she nearly died. Fabian, who hadn't tasted milk in five years, also donated blood.

Later, the donors would learn that the agents were not from the Red Cross and that the blood was not going to wounded Sudanese, but was being sold to Kenyan hospitals for profit.

For Fabian, the only bright spot in Kakuma was the church group that met together every Wednesday, Friday and Sunday. He immediately got involved and joined the refugee choir that was established several years earlier, he was told, by a refugee who had since left the camp.

There was another choir, too, and the two groups sang at services every Sunday morning. They also accepted invitations to sing at a church at Lokichokio, a Kenyan airport and Red Cross base a few kilometres away from the camp.

"God used the choir as a strong ministry tool," Fabian observes. "We sang at every single service and it gave us all so much joy. People's lives were changed.

"I met refugees in that church who really believed in Jesus. Worshipping together was a wonderful thing. People from many ethnic communities in the camp came together to worship with us."

Fabian was learning a lot about God from the songs, now that he was paying attention to the words.

"Back in Lubumbashi, Michel and Aliston and I used to sing the songs for fun. Now, in the situation I was in, the songs had so much more meaning. I knew Jesus really was there for us—even in the refugee camp."

Every Wednesday, Fabian joined the believers in fasting and praying all day and all night. "We didn't sleep, we just prayed, and not only for ourselves. We kind of forgot about ourselves and began to think of the ministries of God around the world. We prayed for the people who were faithfully spreading His Word, particularly in places where it wasn't easy to preach about Jesus. We prayed for Christians in those situations, too. Most of all, we prayed for Christ to come back soon and end all the suffering."

Mail distribution at Kakuma Refugee Camp took place at 10:00 each morning. For Fabian, it wasn't a time of anticipation because he never received any mail.

One morning, however, he was passing behind a young man who had received a letter and happened to glimpse the handwriting on the envelope. It drew his eyes like a magnet.

His heart began to thump wildly. He blinked hard to clear his vision.

Had he seen right?

The handwriting on the envelope looked familiar. Surely nobody else in the whole world wrote as badly as his brother Michel. Why, his handwriting was a family joke.

And here it was—on the envelope.

"Please," Fabian said, "may I look at that?"

Slowly, he turned the envelope over in his hands.

His eyes found the left-hand corner and the return address. Michel Lwamba, it read. Saskatoon, Saskatchewan, Canada.

"I screamed," Fabian recalls. "I cried. I couldn't believe my eyes. My brother Michel was alive. He was writing to this person in the camp to say he had arrived in Canada and was safe and well."

It was a time of rejoicing for Fabian that evening at Wednesday night worship.

"I just had to get up and testify," he says. "I told them, 'This person you lived with for so many years is my brother. So is Aliston. Gisele is my sister. They are my family. I thought they were all dead.'"

It was a surprise for Fabian's fellow Christians, too. Fabian had never revealed his surname. Now, realizing the two young men they had loved and respected so much were Fabian's brothers, the residents of Kakuma were eager to tell him everything they could about his family members. They even had some photographs of Michel and Aliston, taken while they were in the camp. Fabian was astonished and saddened to see how gaunt and wasted Michel, especially, had become.

But it was a joy-filled day nevertheless, just knowing Michel and Aliston were alive. He couldn't remember ever feeling happier.

He immediately wrote a letter to Michel.

"I am alive and well," Fabian wrote. "Now that I know you are alive, too, I can hang on as long as I have to."

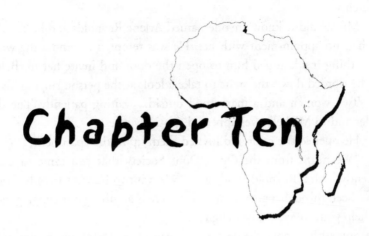

Chapter Ten

BACK IN SASKATOON, MICHEL HELD THE PRECIOUS LETTER CLOSE TO HIS HEART. His eyes filled with tears.

It was a miracle.

Fabian was alive.

"My God!" he exclaimed over and over. "Can this be true?"

He read the letter again. "I am alive," Fabian wrote, "and living in the refugee camp where you were. I am very glad to hear you are still alive, too."

There was no demand, no plea in the letter to do whatever Michel could to get Fabian out of the refugee camp, just reiterations about how glad he was to know Michel and Aliston, Gisele and Sakina were alive.

"That night, I felt as if I were in heaven," Michel says. "I couldn't sleep. I'd been having trouble sleeping before that, but for different reasons. This night, I was ecstatically happy. It was literally like finding a dead person alive."

Another interesting thing happened that day. Michel received unexpected visitors.

When the apartment intercom buzzed, Michel took his time answering it. The people from Immigration Services had advised him not to open the door to anyone he didn't know. "This is not Africa," they said, "and your apartment is in a rougher area of the city. Be sure you have an appointment with the person at your door."

Michel asked twice who was there. His visitor said she was Arlene Reynolds, the pastor of Trinity United Church and that she had two other people from the church with her.

Michel didn't know anyone named Arlene Reynolds and he certainly knew he had no appointment with her. He was tempted to ignore the woman, but something inside urged him to open the door and invite her in. Before doing so, he tiptoed down the stairs to take a look at the person ringing his doorbell.

Two women and a man stood outside, waiting patiently. The three were older and to Michel's eyes appeared relatively safe.

He opened the door and invited them up to the apartment.

"We heard from the Open Door Society that you came to Canada just recently," Mrs. Reynolds told him. "We want to be your friends. I'm sure you have been through a great deal and if there is anything our congregation can do to help you, we would be delighted."

Something about the pastor's demeanour and her conversation told Michel he could trust her. He shared a bit of his story and he told Arlene about the letter he had received from Fabian that very morning and about his joy at learning his brother was alive.

The pastor was deeply moved. "Let me talk to our church committee," she said. "Perhaps we can find a way to bring your brother here to Saskatoon."

Michel was grateful for their interest, but he didn't hold out much hope. "Anything your church can do," he said, "we will appreciate."

To his amazement, Arlene Reynolds returned a couple of weeks later with a large hamper of food and gifts for the family and the news that Trinity United Church was eager to sponsor Fabian so he could rejoin his family.

The paperwork began immediately, but the process was a lengthy one. Through it all, God continued to teach Michel that He was in control of the situation.

"God showed me that even though He allowed the things that happened in my life, He could put the same power to work for me that divided the Red Sea long ago so the Israelites could walk across," he says.

In agreeing to sponsor Fabian, Trinity Church discovered they were getting more than they bargained for. They could afford to sponsor Fabian, but Edwine came as a surprise. Of course, Fabian refused to leave her behind. "She's my only family right now," he said.

Fortunately, the Government of Canada stepped in and sponsored Edwine. They recommended that she be immediately enrolled in therapy when she settled in Canada. As it turned out, Edwine refused to go to any office for therapy sessions, but the ladies of Trinity Church did an admirable job in helping her deal with her trauma. Being reunited with Michel and the other family members went a long way toward her healing.

While the congregation of Trinity United Church was working to bring Fabian to Canada, Michel was finding help from another Saskatoon church to bring Betty to this country.

During a tour of the city with Sarath Hem from the Open Door Society, Michel asked if there were any churches close to the apartment where he and his family were living. Hem was only familiar with his own church, which conducted services in the Chinese language.

Michel's second question was whether or not Sarath knew of any other Zaireans in Saskatoon. Sarath offered to check around.

A week or so later he came up with the name of a Zairean man who attended Emmanuel Baptist Church. Unfortunately, it was clear across the city from where Michel lived.

"I don't have a car to drive you to church," the African told Michel, "but I have a friend who might give you a lift."

The friend was Allan Barr, who got in touch with Michel the very same evening he was contacted and invited the Lwamba family for dinner.

Allan's wife Barb speaks fluent French, so the conversation that night was comfortable and lively. The Barrs wanted to know all about Africa and were especially interested in hearing about the Lwambas' experiences in Zaire. Michel told them about locating Fabian and Betty and about his need to find a way to bring his wife to Canada.

Allan offered to introduce Michel to Cal Malena, the senior pastor of Emmanuel Church. "Cal will help you find a way to bring Betty here," Allan said, "and he'll also find someone to give you a ride to church whenever you want."

Within days of meeting Malena, Michel was informed that Emmanuel Church would indeed sponsor Betty. His spirits were high as he and Cal set off together for the Immigration Canada office to make the application. But his hopes were dashed when he learned that Betty was not eligible to immigrate to Canada because she was not a conventional refugee living in a refugee camp.

Cal picked up the rejected application and put his hand on Michel's shoulder. "Let me see what I can do," he said.

Michel was too numb to do anything more than nod his head.

After some discussion and consultation, Cal was able to persuade the immigration officials that Betty's case qualified under the status of family reunification. As such, all she needed to be able to come to Canada was a valid passport.

In August, 1997, Betty, Rodrigue and the newest Lwamba, baby Micheline, arrived. In preparation, Michel had secured more spacious quarters in a townhouse complex nearer to Emmanuel Church.

Betty's flight was scheduled for Calgary, Alberta, and Cal drove Michel, Fabian and the girls the 600 kilometres to meet her there.

The flight arrived and the group waited impatiently for their first sight of Michel's wife and children.

Betty was the last person to come through the gate. Cal remembers the impact she made, looking regal and sedate in a gold-coloured traditional African dress, her hair beautifully arranged. Rodrigue, in a little white suit, was at her side.

Two women standing nearby murmured, "I wonder who she is."

"Probably a diplomat's wife," the other one guessed.

Cal found the remarks rather amusing. "They had no idea," he says, "that all of Betty's earthly possessions were contained in the one handbag she carried on her arm."

Fabian and Edwine arrived in July of the following year. They had to remain in Kakuma Refugee Camp for another 12 months while the necessary arrangements were made. It was almost 10 years since Fabian had seen his brothers. He hardly recognized them. Aliston had grown a moustache. When they were separated in 1989, he was only 13.

Fabian's arrival in Saskatoon was very different from Michel's.

"By the time we reached Canada, I was mentally and physically broken," Michel recalls. "I don't know exactly what happened, because in the refugee camp, I was very strong. Maybe it was the realization when I left Kenya that I would never see my home or my relatives again. Aliston and Gisele and Sakina and I arrived in Canada knowing no one. We started over from scratch in a new culture and an unfamiliar climate. Fabian, on the other hand, had someone to come to and we couldn't wait to see him."

On Fabian's very first Sunday in Canada, Cal invited him and his two brothers to sing during a service at Emmanuel Baptist Church. It was a moving experience for the Lwambas and for the whole congregation. It was also a veiled first glimpse of the ministry for which God had been preparing the brothers from Zaire.

It was as natural as breathing for Michel, Fabian and Aliston to begin singing together again. They soon acquired guitars and often spent whole days just making music. It was profoundly healing.

The music and their joy at being together again compensated in some small measure for their tremendous losses. In praising God for preserving and reuniting them, the brothers experienced a sense of forgiveness that went beyond human comprehension.

Shortly after Fabian's arrival, Trinity United Church, Fabian's sponsor, invited the Lwambas to sing there. Soon other groups were issuing invitations.

The brothers named themselves Krystaal, which is a combination of the Swahili word for "Christ," and "crystal" which symbolized the hope that their lives would be transparent enough for Christ to shine through them and their music.

Everywhere they performed, people were moved, not only by their instrumental and vocal accomplishment, but by the power and the spirit of their songs and the fragments of their story that they shared.

Melodies and lyrics for new songs bubbled like water from a hidden inner source. Fabian would often hear a new song in his head in the middle of the night. He knew by the sheer beauty of it that the music came from God.

"I first began hearing music in my dreams in the refugee camp after Jesus became so meaningful in my life," he says. "It was a gift from God then and it is a gift from God now. In the camp, hearing music like that gave me the courage to go on.

"I hear chords...sweet chords that I wish I could play. Often I will wake up and grab my guitar and try to replicate them right there, but I can never make the music sound quite as beautiful as it is in my dreams."

Many of the nocturnal tunes are part of the music repertoire Krystaal sings today.

"We know our music is from God," Michel says. "Everything about it is a miracle. How we learned to play the guitar in the very beginning is a miracle. The way we all feel about music is a miracle. The way people respond to our music is a miracle. There is a power in music that changes lives and because our music springs from what we have experienced, we believe we have something to give to people who are hurting. I can't explain it, but God touches people's hearts with the music He gives us."

It didn't take long for the Lwamba brothers to realize that God was calling them to a full-time music ministry. They weren't exactly sure where such a ministry would take them or what they would have to do to get it established, but they determined together to make themselves and their talents available to God and just be obedient to His leading.

While they were working through all this, a friend of Betty's came to visit in Saskatoon. She was Esperance Sabina Mitongo, a beautiful young woman from Lubumbashi with whom Betty had gone to school. Like Gilbert Lwamba, Sabina's father worked for the Zairean government and came into conflict with Mobutu's corrupt regime. When her father was killed, the remaining family members ran for their lives.

Sabina lived in a refugee camp near Mombasa, Kenya, for some time before immigrating to South Dakota with her brothers. It was there they received word that their mother had been shot in the family home and that their sister was also murdered.

Sabina and Betty had kept contact all through those difficult refugee years and now Sabina was coming to visit her childhood friend.

Sabina and Fabian met, fell in love and were married.

Little by little, the Lwambas were able to piece together their family's tragic story. Following the disappearance of Michel and Fabian from Lubumbashi, Gilbert and his wife were seized, taken from their home and presumably murdered. So were Edwine's brother Mokili and his family. Mobutu's men seized the family mansion in Lubumbashi and destroyed all the furniture and the Lwambas' personal belongings. The house was commandeered by the government. Being too fine and valuable a building to be vandalized or demolished, the building became an official government residence.

Gilbert's bank accounts and those of his children were confiscated. His holdings in Burundi were also seized. The family home there was destroyed during the ensuing war.

It is estimated that as many as 120 members of the extended Lwamba family were massacred by Mobutu's regime. Many died in prison where they were starved, tortured or beaten to death.

The realization was devastating—so devastating that the brothers were almost reluctant to search for surviving family members. But urging them on was the thought that a brother or sister might be alive and suffering as they themselves had. They began by contacting the International Red Cross, which has access to the refugee lists in all the camps, inquiring if anyone with the Lwamba name had shown up.

Ironically, it was a very different source that brought the news that their brother George and his family were alive and living in Kenya.

On the afternoon of Fabian's first Sunday in Saskatoon, Cal Malena took the Lwamba family to Christopher Lake where the Baptist churches of Saskatchewan have a fine camp facility. A youth camp was in progress and Cal introduced the brothers to Ali, the camp cook. Ali was a Sudanese man who had spent time in a refugee camp himself.

"Did you say your name is Lwamba?" he inquired. "I know of a Lwamba."

"What's his name?"

"George."

"You know George Lwamba?" Cal asked. "These guys have a brother George."

"I don't know him myself, but I have a friend in Edmonton who knows a George Lwamba. My friend was in a refugee camp at Dadaab, near Mombasa."

Michel, Fabian and Aliston were ecstatic. Could this George Lwamba be their brother?

Ali wrote down his friend's address and a few days later, Michel and Aliston accepted Cal's offer to use his car and headed for Edmonton to investigate.

They located the address and knocked on the door.

"I understand you know George Lwamba," Michel said to the fellow who opened the door.

The man hesitated. "Why are you looking for him?" he asked.

"We think he's our brother."

The man's face brightened. "I didn't want to tell you his whereabouts until I knew why you wanted him," he said.

Michel appreciated the caution. He knew that he and his brothers would need to be equally wise when they made contact with George. To convince him it was indeed his brothers making contact, they sent George a photograph of the three of them with a letter.

Not many weeks later, George responded. The congregation of Emmanuel Baptist agreed to sponsor him and his family to be reunited with the rest of the Lwambas in Canada. In the meantime, the family in Saskatoon began sending a little bit of money each month so George and his family could move out of the camp and rent a place in Nairobi while they waited for the immigration process to work through.

As Michel explains, "Once you have been through the painful experience of living in a refugee camp, the first thing you want to do for someone in a camp is get them out, especially if they have children."

During the Mobutu years, George was a professor of commerce at a small college in Lubumbashi. He also served as assistant pastor in a Christian church there. Immediately after the student massacre in 1989, he and his wife Philomene and their four children went into hiding. Having been active in a democratic political movement during his own student career, he knew he would be a likely target for Mobutu's revenge.

George, Philomene, Nicole, Cecile and twin boys Fabian and Houston arrived in Saskatoon in December of 1999. Like Michel and Aliston, they arrived on a bitterly cold day. The weather was a shock to their African systems. George stepped off the plane wearing the traditional long African dress made of cotton. Bob Nylen, one of the men from Emmanuel Church who had come to meet the family, saw how violently George was shivering and quickly wrapped his own coat around him. The gesture of kindness was a symbol of the loving care and acceptance the family would experience in their new Canadian home.

Chapter Eleven

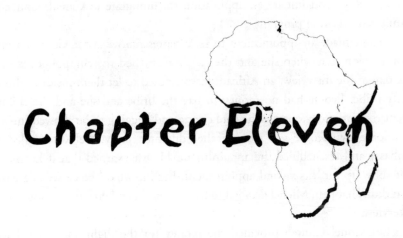

THROUGH THE RED CROSS, THE LWAMBAS LEARNED THAT THEIR SISTERS LEONIE and Julienne were also alive and living in a refugee camp in eastern Kenya. The brothers approached the process of making contact with the same delicacy they exercised with George.

Once Leonie saw the photograph of the men who claimed to be her brothers and recognized their faces, she was overjoyed.

Leonie and her husband were both teachers in the Kisingani region of northeastern Congo. Like their fellow teachers, they had not been paid for more than two years. Leonie's husband, who was also the principal of a school, became outspoken in his demands on behalf of the teachers for their rightfully earned wages. His demands came to the attention of Mobutu's government, which immediately put him and his family in danger. All seven of them ran for their lives to Kenya where they ended up in a refugee camp. Later on, the husband received word that some of his family members had been killed and that his father and mother were in serious trouble. He left Leonie and the children in the camp and went back to try and bring his parents out of Congo to Kenya. He never returned.

Leonie was left in the camp with their five children. Julienne was there, too, but she had fallen in love with a man from Burundi and chose to stay with him in Africa. Leonie, however, was eager to join the family in Canada.

Knowing how vulnerable women in refugee camps are to violence and rape, Leonie's brothers were impatient to get her into a safer situation. From their meagre income, they sent money every month so Leonie could rent a small apartment in Nairobi. Michel also instructed his sister to go to the Canadian embassy there and initiate an application to immigrate to Canada under the family reunification program.

Leonie made an appointment to see a representative at the Canadian High Commission, but when she and the children reached the compound gates on the day of the interview, an African guard refused to let them inside without a hefty bribe. Leonie had no money to pay the bribe and she and the children spent the entire day outside the gate crying and begging to be allowed in.

Somehow Leonie got word of her dilemma to Michel who called the embassy and rescheduled the appointment. He was warned that if Leonie did not show up for this second appointment, her file would be closed. To ensure that didn't happen, Michel decided to fly to Nairobi and go with his sister to the interview.

Emmanuel Church provided the money for the flight and Michel went armed with written assurance from Mount Royal Mennonite Church in Saskatoon that they would sponsor Leonie and her children.

When Michel arrived in Nairobi, the only way he could get in touch with Leonie was via her neighbour's phone.

"I am at the Hilton Hotel," he told Leonie when she finally came to the telephone. "Can you and the children meet me here?"

"How will we get there?" Leonie wondered.

"Take a taxi."

"But I don't have any money."

"I'll pay for it when you get here."

Michel waited and watched. Thirty, then 40 minutes elapsed before he finally saw a little knot of people enter the lobby and wander uncertainly toward the reception desk. The woman in the group looked like Leonie, but surely those weren't her children. The oldest ones were young adults. And how shabbily dressed they all were. And who, exactly, was the man with them?

It was indeed Leonie and when she saw Michel, she leaped in the air for joy. Had it not been for the photograph he sent, she would never have recognized him. The brother and sister hadn't seen each other for at least 15 years. When Michel and Fabian left Zaire, Leonie had only two children. Now she had five and the oldest boy, Steve, was already well into his teens.

The children clamoured around Michel, hugging him and calling him "Uncle." Leonie just stood there looking at him.

Finally Michel remembered the man with them. He was still waiting patiently.

"This is the cab driver who brought us here," Leonie explained.

Michel thanked the man and paid him, then turned back to Leonie. "We'll go up to my room."

The hotel desk clerk overheard him. "No," he said, eyeing the way Leonie and her children were dressed, "these people can go no further into the hotel."

"I'm sorry, but you must let them in," Michel said firmly. "This is my sister and her family."

The seven of them went to the room and for a long time, all Leonie and Michel could do was look at one another and cry. It was a highly emotional moment for both of them.

Finally Michel had the presence of mind to ask, "Have you eaten today?"

"Oh, yes," they all assured him, but he really didn't believe it.

"Let's go down to the restaurant," he proposed.

When the food came to the table, the children looked at one another in disbelief. Michel wondered how long it had been since they saw that much food at one time or if indeed, they ever had. He could see them blinking hard, as if they thought it was all a dream and the banquet spread before them might disappear.

"Go ahead and eat," he said after they had prayed over the food. It was a joy for him just to watch the children eat and see the sparkle the good food brought to their eyes.

Michel ate sparingly and deliberately left some food on his plate. When the children had eaten everything else, they asked if they could finish his.

"Of course," he said. How he wished he could take them all back to Canada with him immediately, but he knew they would have to work through the process.

Michel accompanied Leonie to her appointment with the Immigration Canada representative at the Canadian High Commission. Her application to be reunited with the family in Canada was approved. The next step was a battery of medical checkups.

For the next two weeks, Michel devoted himself to making the little family happy. He bought them clothing and shoes. The younger children had never worn shoes before. They had a difficult time adjusting.

Leonie's eldest son, Steve, had been sleeping on a mattress of bare metal springs with only a thin cloth spread over the coils for protection. Michel bought him a real mattress. He also got Steve a little television set.

"Steve loved soccer," Michel says. "He loved it so much, he would sneak up to the window of a house where the people inside were watching a game on television. As soon as they saw him at the window, they would close it. I bought him an inexpensive little television so he could watch his beloved sport whenever he wanted."

It made Michel so happy to see Leonie's children smiling and joyful. The change in them was dramatic and he knew why. It was because they now had hope.

It would be two years before Leonie and her family finally made it to Saskatoon. In the meantime, the family in Canada faithfully sent $150 every month for her living. It wasn't always easy to find the extra money, but they never once considered it a sacrifice.

"We were living privileged lives in Canada, knowing that our children had everything they needed and would always be looked after," Michel explains. "It made the situation of our nieces and nephews all the more critical. We knew that on her own Leonie would never be able to move, she would never get a job, she would never be able to survive. We knew we had to do everything we could. That small amount—which is considered nothing in this country—was like gold in Kenya. It allowed Leonie to feed and clothe her children and put a roof over their heads."

As the Lwamba family in Canada waited for Leonie to join them, they collectively and individually reconnected with one another here and made the necessary adjustments to a new life and a new culture. More and more, they were able to look back on their life experiences and see how God was clearly at work at every turn. They sensed a great excitement and anticipation for what was ahead.

"In the refugee camp, I sometimes blamed God for my circumstance," Michel recalls. "I would say, 'Why am I in this situation? Am I being punished for something? Why am I being tested beyond what I can endure when You say in Your Word that You will never let that happen?'

"God rebuked me. In my heart I heard Him telling me, 'This is not more than your faith can handle. I am preparing you.' If I had not heard that, I might have hanged myself—or ended my life some other way there in the camp. But I was able to endure, able to keep on standing to the end because I took God at His word. I believed He was preparing me for something else. I had no idea what it was and certainly never imagined that we would be brought back together like this.

"In our early lives, we were at the top in terms of privilege and prosperity. Then we were dragged to the very bottom, but God came into our lives and lifted us up again. We know He did it for a reason."

The reason became more and more evident as Krystaal continued to receive invitations to perform in churches and public events around Saskatoon. They were somewhat surprised to find that, besides being moved by their music, audiences were deeply impacted by the snippets they told of their life experiences.

They hesitated to tell too much, thinking no one would want to hear of the horrors and tragedy they had endured. And when Michel was approached soon after his arrival in Saskatoon to have Krystaal's story documented in a book, he hedged—for a number of reasons. The main reason was that the experiences were still too recent to talk about. The sorrow was too raw, the wounds too fresh to be probed.

But as time went on and the men realized how deeply people were affected by hearing what God had done in their lives, they warmed to the idea of writing a book.

Chapter Twelve

ONE DAY EVERYTHING CAME TO A HEAD. MICHEL SENSED GOD SAYING VERY clearly to him, "Michel, this is not your story. This is My story. I created you and I brought you to where you are so you can tell people about all that I have done for you. I want them to see My power and My glory. It is time for the story to be told."

Thus began a series of weekly sessions that continued for well over a year. Michel, Fabian and Aliston started from the very beginning and recounted everything they could remember about their family, life in Zaire under Mobutu's corrupt regime, the events that led to their escape and incarceration in refugee camps and ultimately, how they were reunited in Canada. Dealing with the memories was often painful, but as the weeks went by, an interesting phenomenon took place. At one point, Michel remarked that his shoulders always felt lighter after the weekly session. It was apparent that verbalizing the pain and trauma was bringing healing.

The title chosen for the book was *Keep on Standing*. It was also the name of a song Krystaal had written, expressing the need to keep on standing firm, even when the way gets rough, because—as He promises in Scripture—God will ultimately triumph and bring good out of evil for those who love Him.

The book proved to be an effective key for opening doors to ministry. It opened so many doors, in fact, that the brothers would later remark, "If we had known how God would use our story to impact people's lives, we would have come running to have it written, rather than avoiding it for so long."

Another thing that gave Krystaal's musical career a boost was appearing on "100 Huntley Street," a daily television program produced in Ontario by Crossroads Christian Communications. This was the first time any of them had ever been on television and they were extremely nervous. They sang a couple of songs and related the bare bones of their story. Even before the show was over, the phones began ringing. Listeners wanted more information about Krystaal and their music.

Following the segment, Reverend Norman MacLaren, vice-president of Crossroads Christian Communications, remarked on air, "If I was a pastor—and I used to be—I would be clamouring to have these guys come to my church. They are the sweetest spirited men you will ever meet. What a powerful, powerful story and what a life of miracles God has brought to these precious brothers."

The Lwambas found strong support from their home church, Emmanuel Baptist, as well. Several people there played a key role in helping them connect with individuals and organizations that would ultimately advance their ministry. One was Terry Summach, a generous supporter on a number of fronts; another was Emmanuel's senior pastor, Cal Malena.

Cal and his family had recently returned from a sabbatical leave, part of which was spent in Belgium working in church ministry in the city of Liège with Patrick and Ria Deneut. Patrick was on staff with Canadian Baptist Ministries as a church planter in Liege and was later appointed CBM manager for the Francophonie, responsible for development and strategic planning and assisting the national churches in French-speaking places like Rwanda, Congo, France, Belgium and Quebec, Canada.

Having discovered how many Congolese refugees there are in Belgium and the number of Congolese Baptist churches there, Cal recognized a great ministry potential for Krystaal and began making plans for a two-week ministry trip to Belgium for himself and the group. Cal's daughter Beth was spending a year in Belgium, working with the Deneuts and helped to arrange the itinerary.

It was the first time Krystaal had toured outside of Canada and they really had no idea what it would entail. Despite Cal's warning to pack light, they took virtually everything they owned and were forced to spend precious moments at the airport discarding items and repacking only the absolute necessities in their luggage.

In Belgium, the group travelled in a little station wagon that was jammed to the rafters with luggage and passengers: the three Lwambas, Cal and Beth and sometimes Patrick. The instruments and rented sound equipment were strapped to the top of the car on a carrier ingeniously fashioned from broomsticks.

The two weeks were packed with concerts, many of them in churches where Krystaal played to gatherings of 100 or 200 people. Their most enjoyable stops were the concerts in Congolese churches, where the young expatriates, their lively music and their message were enthusiastically received.

Perhaps the most memorable stop on the tour was a jail in Tournai on Easter Sunday.

"We checked in with our instruments and were led into a big room where the prisoners were all gathered," Fabian recalls. "We introduced ourselves and said, 'We have come from Canada to see you guys.' Then we sang a song that talked about joy coming in the morning and how Jesus was raised from the dead at Easter. Black and White, you could just see those men melt. We told them we knew how it felt to be forsaken and rejected, that we were rejected in the refugee camp. We told them how Christ's love embraced us and made us know that we were still valuable to God and they were, too. Then Cal shared a powerful message of hope and acceptance. The men responded in a profound way. Afterward, many came and gave us hugs."

The team had a few tense moments when the event was over and the prisoners filed back to their cells. It took longer than anticipated for the door to open so the Canadians could leave the prison. For Fabian, Michel and Aliston, the old insecurities kicked in. Was this a trick? Were they now prisoners?

After some very anxious moments, the big door finally slid open and they were free.

In the months and years to follow, Krystaal would come to know the true impact their ministry had on the prisoners at Tournai. They still get e-mails from some of the inmates. One wrote recently, "The day you were here was the day I received Christ. I am a changed person now. I worship Jesus Christ."

In 2005, Krystaal paid a return visit to Tournai Prison. The second time was even more emotional than the first. The prison is now a maximum security institution populated with men suffering from all sorts of psychological problems. One was a 24-year-old Rwandan man.

"This kid heard us sing and share our testimony," Michel says. "Afterward, he started telling us about the genocide in Rwanda. 'I was 12 when they brought me to this prison,' he told us. 'I haven't seen my dad in all that time. I want to see him. I just want to know if he's alive. Could you go see him for me?' It was heartbreaking."

Another unforgettable experience was meeting up with Frank, a university friend from Lubumbashi. After the massacre, Michel and Fabian lost track of Frank, so seeing him again in Belgium was a major event. Frank, a Christian now living in Brussels, found Krystaal's website on the Internet and e-mailed them some months before the Belgium trip. Michel told him they would be in touch.

They called Frank from the train station in Brussels and their friend met them there. It was a deeply emotional reunion. The four young men from Congo threw their arms around one another and laughed and cried and prayed right there in the middle of the street.

Later, Frank took the Lwambas to his home and cooked them a Congolese meal.

Having observed the impact of Krystaal's ministry in Belgium, Patrick Deneut could see other ministry opportunities, especially in Quebec and French Canada. The one drawback was that the brothers were committed to conducting their ministry in English.

"We need people to minister in French," Patrick observed. "Are you sure you don't have any French-speaking relatives?"

"As a matter of fact, we do," Michel replied. "We have a brother George, who is still very francophone. George has experience in Bible teaching and spent time as an assistant pastor in Zaire, though he's more of an evangelist. He would like to do some preaching in Canada, but he doesn't speak English well enough."

Patrick's eyes brightened. "You say he speaks French?"

"Almost exclusively."

"We would love to have him join us. Maybe we can arrange something."

Soon afterward, Patrick and Ria spent a sabbatical year in Saskatoon where they became very well acquainted with George and Philomene Lwamba. The Deneuts and the entire Lwamba family met together regularly during that year for Bible studies in French. Patrick and George took turns teaching.

Thus, the plans were put in motion for George to become a church planter in Montréal with Canadian Baptist Ministries. Krystaal went on a concert tour to eastern Canada and took George along. In Montreal, he preached in a number of churches and became acquainted with some of the people there.

In the meantime, his younger brothers continued to immerse themselves in music. They were developing an appealing eclectic style that blended African and North American music.

"Music has so much to do with culture," Fabian explains. "We never wanted to be identified with just one song or one type of music. Our goal early on was to reach all cultures and all nations. That goal influences the kind of music we play.

"When we came to Canada, we brought our African musical culture with us. We brought *soukouss* or Afro-jazz, which is a fusion of North American music and African jazz. It has the strong influence of African drums and percussion. Sometimes we put in a little jazz piano and saxophone, too."

This unique music style was evident in the first CD Krystaal released. Entitled "Little Child," it was produced in Saskatoon by Lyndon Smith and Kent Regier and launched on April 29, 2002. Many of the songs expressed the brothers' raw emotions and the deep sorrow that lingered in their hearts.

"We were fresh from Africa and we were still crying," Michel observes. "When you hear the music, you immediately know we were trying to say something. The message is strong and clear. One song says, 'They just killed my father.' You can hear the sorrowing in the song; you can feel the pain. We spoke of what was in our hearts. In the song, a little girl is talking. Her words were us speaking. What she said was what we knew to be real. It is what we ourselves experienced. When you are mourning, what comes out of your mouth is what is in your heart. The cry of your heart is a cry for help."

Another song, "Nobody's Home," stemmed from the brothers' loneliness for their parents. Understandably, they were often overwhelmed with moments of wistfulness and melancholy. They wished they could hear their father's voice, feel their mother's caress. They wished their mother and father could see the stalwart men they had become.

"Nobody's Home" grew out of a song Michel remembered his mother singing to him when he was a little boy. It is a lullaby, a song village mothers sing to calm their crying children. It talks about the fact that nobody in the village is home. With their mother now gone, the little lullaby took on much deeper meaning for Aliston, Fabian and Michel. Not only were all the village people physically gone, so were Gilbert and Edwine. They were not just away on vacation; they were gone for good.

The songs on the CD were all written in English, even though none of the three were particularly fluent in the language yet. Getting the message across was the most important thing, more important even than grammar, smooth phrasing or perfect rhyme schemes. In later years, they would try to rewrite some of those early songs to bring them up to music industry standards, but somehow, the songs lost their passion. The rewrites were never used.

Krystaal's first concert invitation to the United States came from Boston. It was issued by Pastor Jared Alongecha, who had heard them perform on their eastern Canadian tour. Pastor Jared heads an evangelism ministry that organizes events in Africa and the US, including a large youth rally each summer.

The Lwambas invited two Saskatoon musician friends to accompany them: pianist and vocal artist Donna Tiezen and drummer Paul Benjamin. Cal Malena rented a car for them to drive to Boston.

When the group arrived at the US border crossing in southern Saskatchewan, things got complicated. Being Canadian citizens, Paul and Donna had no problem getting into the United States. The same was not true for the Lwambas.

"Where were you born?"

"Congo," Michel answered, "but we live in Canada now."

"I need to see your Canadian passports."

"We don't have Canadian passports. We haven't been in Canada long enough to become citizens."

"Sorry, we can't allow you into the United States."

"We have our landed immigrant papers," Michel persisted, handing the officer the precious documents.

The border guard scanned the papers. "These only allow you to stay in Canada. They don't allow you to enter the United States. If you were coming from a Commonwealth country, it would be different, but you're not. You'll have to go back."

"But we're on our way to sing at a Christian gathering in Boston. Can't you make an exception?"

"Sorry, no."

"Is there anything we can do?"

"You're still technically citizens of Congo. If you had Congolese passports, you would be allowed entry into the United States."

"How do we get Congolese passports?"

"You have to go to Ottawa. By the way, you'll also need visas."

"Where do we get those?"

"In Ottawa."

Thoroughly discouraged, the group turned the car around and headed back to the Canada Customs building where they explained to the officials why they were being refused entry into the US.

As they were about to leave, one guard called them aside.

"Do you guys believe God or human beings set up these borders?"

"Human beings."

"Do you believe you've been called by God to do this ministry thing?"

"Yes."

"Then what are you going to do about it?"

"I don't know," Michel replied.

"Are you going to go back home and sleep? Or are you going to find another way to get those passports and do what God has called you to do?"

"We're going home to find a way."

The border guard's bracing challenge rang in the brothers' ears all the way back to Saskatoon.

When they got home, they phoned Pastor Jared and explained their predicament. Since he had already advertised that a band from Canada would be headlining at the meetings, he was reluctant to have them cancel.

"If you can get to Ottawa," he said, "I will wire you the money to pay for the passports."

Michel, Fabian and Aliston got into the rented car and began the 3046 kilometre drive to Ottawa. They went alone this time; Donna and Paul were unable to give the extra time that the extended trip demanded.

The first thing the brothers did when they arrived in Ottawa was pick up the money Pastor Jared had wired. They went to find the Zairean embassy. Going there was the last thing the boys wanted to do, but they had no choice.

Interestingly, it was a Swahili-speaking man from Lubumbashi who assisted them. He recognized the Lwamba name and did everything he could to help.

The three filled out the required application forms, paid the money and the very next day received their brand new Congolese passports.

The next stop was the American embassy where they applied for visitors' visas.

"Why do you want to go to the United States?"

"We are going to Boston to sing at a Christian conference."

"Can you verify that?"

Michel showed the man the paper with Pastor Jared's telephone number. The official immediately placed a telephone call while the Lwambas waited on pins and needles. Time was getting away. They were already a day late for the conference.

The official returned. "Come with me, please," he said, opening the door to another room.

Somewhat apprehensive, the brothers stepped inside. There were several people in the room. All watched them closely.

"Sing something," one of them ordered.

The brothers looked at one another. "Let's sing 'I Must Have Jesus,'" Michel suggested and they proceeded to do so.

When they were done, the officer said, "Yes, you are singers. Here's your visa."

Being part of the conference in Boston was a blessing and God used Krystaal's music ministry there in a significant way. It would be a place to which they would return again and again.

Back in Saskatoon, Cal Malena was beginning a three-year term as president of Canadian Baptist Ministries in Canada. At his suggestion, the Lwambas were invited to attend the conference that is held at the Banff Springs Hotel each year for pastors from the Baptist Union of Western Canada and the North American Baptist Conference of Canada.

Krystaal provided an evening of music for the pastors and their guests and the exposure was invaluable. Church leaders from across the country listened to the brothers' music and heard their dramatic testimony. Many came to them afterward to book a concert in their church.

At another CBM board meeting that was hosted by Baptists in Saskatoon and held at the Christopher Lake Camp facility, Krystaal again led the worship. Here CBM board members from across Canada heard their music. It was at this event that Krystaal met Gordon King, then director of support services for Canadian Baptist Ministries. King would later become director of The Sharing Way, the relief and development arm of CBM around the world. He invited Krystaal to Toronto to do a series of special presentations in the Baptist churches in the area.

The arrangements were quickly put in place and Krystaal spent three full weeks performing in Toronto and being hosted by King and his Rwandan wife.

Gordon King came to the position at CBM by way of World Vision, with whom he had worked for several years. He immediately saw the potential for Krystaal and World Vision to work co-operatively and made the necessary connections for the brothers to perform at a World Vision event. The response was overwhelming. So were the invitations that followed.

With invitations now coming from all over North America, the Lwambas realized that they needed to take a hard look at where they were going. They were confident that God wanted to use them in full-time music ministry. This was also their desire, but they realized the need to be professional about their music.

They also had to consider their families. By now Fabian and Sabina had a little boy, Gilbert, and a brand new baby girl, Joellyn. Michel and Betty had four children. So many of their invitations were coming from eastern Canada that the men were constantly travelling between Saskatoon and somewhere far away. They desperately wanted to be in a situation where they could be home at night with their families wherever possible.

Income was another consideration. Krystaal was doing well in Saskatoon in terms of recognition and bookings, but the income generated mainly from church appearances wasn't enough to support two growing families and Aliston. Going to larger conferences for a week at a time offered more in the way of remuneration, but travel was expensive and time consuming.

The men were spending two-thirds of their time performing in the east and coming home only for breaks. Whenever they went, they drove because it was too expensive to ship their instruments and sound equipment by plane. The drive to Toronto alone was three days each way.

It was obvious to the brothers that if they wanted to pursue a professional music career and spend time with their families, they needed to be closer to the heart of the Canadian music industry. It seemed that they had no other option but to move to Toronto.

Chapter Thirteen

IN THE MIDST OF THESE DELIBERATIONS, KRYSTAAL RELEASED A SECOND CD. This one was entitled "Keep on Standing" and contained many new songs. The CD was produced by Lyndon Smith and recorded by Daryl Pierce and had a very different tone from "Little Child."

"Our crying was done," Fabian explains, "and we had gained some courage. We were saying, 'Here we are, God. What next?' God had taken us from the refugee camp and re-established us, giving us a new home. We wondered if there were other people experiencing parallel circumstances—difficulties, sorrow, tragedy and hardships in their lives—who might be encouraged and given hope by the message in our songs."

The new CD featured songs that expressed a sense of confidence and stability, of belonging to a new land. It also had some African tunes and highlighted the artistry of guitarist Jay Buckner and Sheldon Corbett on keyboards.

The overall theme for "Keep on Standing" came out of a passage of Scripture that Michel read shortly after arriving in Saskatoon.

"In the passage, God basically said to Israel, 'Wherever your foot steps, that land will I give you.' I felt He was saying the same thing to us. We had left Africa; He was giving this new land to us and He wanted us to contribute to this new society. Everything had changed for us. We had a new home; we had friends. We were no longer running away; we were stable. We had a band and a home church that believed in us and our work and embraced us wholeheartedly. We needed to do more than just keep on standing; we needed to move on."

The new CD was released on April 29, 2003. The title song, "Keep on Standing," would go on to win several music industry awards.

In the meantime, preparations were underway for the Lwamba family to move to Toronto. George received the invitation to become a church planter in Montréal, with an eye toward establishing a congregation among African and Caribbean refugee and immigrant peoples. His acceptance was one more incentive for the men and their families to head east. After being separated for so long and then reunited by God's grace, the Lwamba family did not want to be apart again. They wanted to stay as close to one another as possible.

Yet Michel, Fabian and Aliston did not feel the motivation to relocate in Montréal with George. Instead, they felt God urging them to develop their music as an English language ministry outside a francophone society. They were working very hard at changing their orientation from being French speaking to becoming anglophone.

In early August of 2003, the Lwambas packed up everything they owned, including their new CD and 1500 or so copies of their book, *Keep on Standing*, and set out for Toronto. On August 8, they pulled into a park in Windsor to celebrate little Gilbert's fourth birthday with a barbecue.

"Leaving Saskatoon was very hard," Fabian recalls. "We had so many good friends there and a church and a support network. We had people who helped us and prayed for us. When our babies were born, they threw baby showers and gave us gifts. After all those years of running and the years on the camps, we had found a place to call home. We were well established in Saskatoon. Michel and Aliston had been there seven years; I was there five. It was hard to pull up our roots and start all over again."

"As a matter of fact," he adds, "we still call Saskatoon home. When anyone asks where we came from, we don't say Congo or Zaire, we say Saskatoon, Saskatchewan."

If the physical process of pulling up stakes was hard, the psychological and emotional adjustment to a mega-urban centre was even harder. Toronto just did not feel like home.

Initially, the family moved into a townhouse together in Scarborough. It was a six-hour drive from Montréal, but almost every weekend would find the Lwambas in George's church, helping with the ministry and music. Sometimes they combined the visit with a concert in some other church in the area.

George poured himself into Breath of Life Church, often using his own funds to help it grow. The congregation also received monthly support from CBM and specifically, Emmanuel Baptist Church in Saskatoon. The congregation of Haitians, Rwandans, Congolese and others grew quickly. Most were refugees.

"For refugees in this country, the church plays more than a spiritual role," Michel points out. "For Africans, especially, family is a very strong part of their native culture. They are used to living with relatives in their home. Now they come to this country and find themselves with no one. Maybe they lost their family. The only place where they can get connected to a family is in church.

"Breath of Life Church gives them the sense of family they need. People come and worship together; they sing songs in Swahili, in Spanish, in Québécois. They have a little meal at the end of the service; they share common experiences and help each other.

"When we sing that 'Joy comes in the morning,' the message resonates with them because they know we've been there. One will say, 'My brother was killed in the violence.' Many of them have a hard time letting go of the past. Others are feeling alienated and lost because they are living in a society that moves so fast they can't catch up to it."

The Lwambas were experiencing some of those same feelings themselves in Toronto. Compared to Saskatoon with its 200,000 or so people, Toronto was a metropolis where everyone was busy. If the phone rang, it was always business. No one ever called just to say, "Hi, how are you guys doing today?" The men longed for someone to phone and say, "Would you like to come for coffee?" Or, "We're going to play a little pick-up basketball. Do you want to come?"

Michel's children found it strange to be attending a multicultural school. "Dad," one of them said, "there are Black people in our school." Back in Saskatoon, they were the only Black children sitting in the desks.

Even relating to a new church was difficult. For a long time, the family drifted from church to church, not wanting to settle into any particular one. They still considered Emmanuel Baptist to be their home church. It seemed to them that they were on the road—just travelling—and would be going home to Saskatoon soon.

Despite all that, Michel, Fabian and Aliston knew they couldn't sit idle and wallow in nostalgia. They were in Toronto to further their music and if they wanted to survive in the competitive environment and develop any kind of professional career, they needed to get at it. They continued to believe God had called them to a music ministry; they wanted to be ready and available for the opportunities He provided.

Their prayer was: "God, we want to take this city by storm with the message of peace and reconciliation. We don't know how we'll do it. Everything is so flashy in the big city. Please show us the next step."

For the first six months, very little happened. Minimal work came Krystaal's way and it was a very stressful time financially. The family desperately needed income to pay the rent and cover their living expenses, but at the same time, they didn't want friends back home in Saskatoon to know how dire their situation was. It was doubly frustrating to have a garage full of books and CDs and nobody knowing about them or wanting them.

The brothers took a first step by reconnecting with the only organization they knew, Canadian Baptist Ministries.

The CBM board wrote a letter of recommendation, introducing Krystaal to all the churches in Ontario and Québec. The French Baptist Association did the same thing and eventually, invitations began to trickle in. For the first year and a half, the men were kept occupied singing in CBM churches.

They used their book, *Keep on Standing*, as an introduction to pastors of other denominations. Once the ministers read the story and became aware of Krystaal's music and their ministry ambitions, they were eager to have the group come and perform.

It was slow going, but gradually things picked up. The young men raised their profile some more by arranging for an assortment of television appearances in Toronto and the surrounding area.

Eventually, another invitation came from Pastor Jared Alongecha in Boston, asking them to come and lead praise and worship at an evangelistic event he was organizing.

Krystaal also made contact with "100 Huntley Street" to see if programmers there were interested in having them on the show again. They were and a taping date was set. With the book and a new CD in hand and a little more camera experience under their belts, Michel, Fabian and Aliston were much more comfortable on air than the first interview.

They led with their signature song "Keep on Standing," and were thrilled to hear that the moment they finished singing, the telephones began to ring "as they had never rung before." There was such a huge response to the song that for 30 minutes after the show was finished, the phone lines were still tied up with people calling. In the month that followed, as a result of their appearance on "100 Huntley Street," Krystaal had 40,000 people e-mail them or visit their new website.

The exposure moved Krystaal's music ministry forward significantly and opened many new doors.

It was about this time that the Lwamba family received word that the immigration process for Leonie and her children was complete. Their arrival date in Canada was set.

Leonie and her five children landed in Toronto one Tuesday afternoon in February, 2004. It was a bitterly cold day. The whole family, including George and Philomene, was there to meet them.

Immigration Canada had booked Leonie into a hotel near the airport, but as soon as the family had checked them in, they took them home to Scarborough. It seemed unbelievable that Leonie was safely in Canada and that they were all together again.

Leonie was overwhelmed. The last time she saw Fabian, he was a teenager babysitting her babies. Now he was married with babies of his own.

The rest of the day was a joyful time of feasting and catching up. There was so much to cry about—their father, their mother, the other girls—and plenty from the past to laugh about.

The intention was to take Leonie and the children back to the hotel, but Leonie didn't want to leave her family just yet. She was exhausted by the trip and from the whole experience; she wanted to spend the night with them. The brothers would be forever grateful that she did.

Early the next morning, Leonie's brothers took her and her children back to the hotel and then on to the airport to catch the connecting flight to Saskatoon. They had been together for less than 24 hours; now they were saying goodbye again. It was terribly difficult.

Leonie arrived in Saskatoon on Wednesday. On Friday, Steve, Leonie's oldest son, called his uncles. He was very excited. He wanted to thank Fabian and Michel for bringing him and his family out of Africa to freedom and plenty in Canada. The people of Mount Royal Mennonite Church had rented a nice apartment for them and to Steve's delight, it was full of furniture. Much of it was stuff that Fabian and Michel left behind when they moved. Each child had his or her own room. There was a dishwasher, a washing machine and all sorts of other gadgets and machines they didn't know how to use.

Steve could hardly contain his joy when he told of being taken to visit the school where he would start classes on Monday. He was delirious with happiness at the prospect of getting an education, something of which he had been deprived for so many years. And, he told his uncles, he had seen the University of Saskatchewan. "When I finish high school, that is where I will go."

The only thing more exciting for Steve than the prospect of going to school was the fact that they had a car. It was an old one that Fabian had left behind for them when he moved, but it was theirs. A car! Imagine!

It was all beyond his wildest expectations. Steve and his family thought they were in heaven.

On Saturday, Steve called again, but no one was home. The family had already left for a weekend tour, so Steve left a message.

On Sunday, Krystaal played a concert with a number of other artists at Peoples Church in Toronto. They came home late, thrilled at the opportunity to be part of the ministry that day.

Too tired to cook, they ordered in pizza.

Partway through the meal, the telephone rang. Michel answered and took the phone upstairs.

When he came down, Fabian knew immediately that something terrible had happened. His brother, who had the heart of a lion, looked devastated.

Michel waited until everyone was finished eating before he told them the news. "Steve died this afternoon."

Leonie and her family were to have been introduced at Mount Royal Church that morning, but Steve wasn't feeling well. "You go without me," he told his mother.

Steve had sickle cell disorder and Leonie, who had lived through enough ups and down with his illness during his 16 years, knew better than to push him. "The rest of us will go," she said. "You stay home and rest."

When Leonie returned from church, she immediately went to Steve's bedroom. Steve kissed his mother and said, "Mom, I'd like to spend some time with you. I want to get up and get dressed. Will you help me shower?"

As Leonie helped him wash up, Steve said, "You know, Mom, the uncles have done a tremendous thing for us. God has done this through them. We mustn't forget God and His way. God has done great, great things for us, Mom," he repeated. "Look where we are. Our dream was to be in a safe place and here we are. Look at all we have."

"Steve, you've never talked to me like this before," Leonie said. "What's going on?"

"I'm not feeling well," Steve confessed, "and I feel I need to tell you these things, Mom. Please, let us never forget God. I want to tell my little brothers not to forget God and not to forget to be thankful for the wonderful things He has given us. We have a good place and we're safe now, Mom. But I'm so tired. I want to go to my room and rest now."

When Leonie came to Steve's room a while later, he had passed away.

Doctors believe the fragile state of Steve's red blood cells and the long flight from Kenya, combined with the high excitement, was all too much for his system. Extremes in emotions are profoundly dangerous for sufferers of sickle cell disorder. In fact, given the horrific experiences the family had been through in recent years, it is a miracle Steve lived as long as he did.

The whole family was in shock. Leonie was devastated. She was deeply attached to her oldest son and depended on him. Steve already spoke some English; he was the one she expected would help her make the transition in this strange new land.

Steve's death was extremely difficult for Gisele, who had flown out earlier in the week to help Leonie and her family settle in and navigate their way through prairie Canadian culture. It was doubly difficult given her own sickle cell condition.

There was one consolation for the grieving family. Steve had received Christ into his heart just one month before the family immigrated to Canada. "Mom," he said, "I want to be baptized." And he was.

While losing Steve took a huge toll, life eventually returned to normal for the Lwambas as new opportunities came Krystaal's way. Gordon King from CBM introduced them to a man named Mike Bowman who was head of the artists' association department of World Vision. Bowman informed them that World Vision wanted to contract Krystaal to do music appearances at some of the international aid organization's events. The brothers were delighted. This was exactly in keeping with their original goal of using their music to bring hope to suffering children who had lost their parents to violence, disease and war. They signed a contract and were welcomed to the organization by a letter from Dave Toycen, World Vision's Canadian president and chief executive officer.

Mike Bowman also made arrangements for Krystaal to audition for a performance slot at the 2004 Covenant Awards, sponsored annually by the

Canadian Gospel Music Association, which gives awards to deserving recipients from across the country. The audition was organized by Tom Jackson Productions and the idea was that the group placing first in the audition would perform at the Awards gala.

The Lwambas had no thought of winning. They were just happy to be doing what they loved to do. Therefore, they were shocked when they won the competition and learned they would be performing on stage that very evening in front of what amounted to the entire Canadian music industry.

It was the kind of exposure money can't buy. The audience included representatives from the Canadian Gospel Music Awards, the CMC (Canadian Music Centre), which distributes CDs for Canadian artists, numerous other artist organizations and producers from all levels.

Following their win and the stage performance, Krystaal was inundated not only with requests to perform, but also with invitations to sign with one promotional company or another. They initially signed with Phoenix Five, a company that promised to take their music to radio. Later on, they would connect with the Canadian Music Centre, but in the meantime, the music of Krystaal was playing on the radio across Canada and the United States and steadily gaining recognition and acceptance.

Bowman suggested that Krystaal submit some of their songs to the Maja Awards and the Canadian Gospel Music Awards for consideration. It proved to be a good move. Krystaal netted nominations in 6 categories at the 2004 Maja Awards and won 4 of them. Their song "Keep on Standing" won the Gospel Songwriter of the Year Award. Krystaal also won Group of the Year, Artist of the Year and Album of the Year for "Keep on Standing." They were up against 37 other bands in a very tight competition and rightly considered the wins to be a huge honour. In the history of the Maja Awards, no other artist or group ever won that many awards in one night.

"To have 'Keep on Standing' voted best song of the year for all of Canada was an immense honour," Michel says. "All we could do was praise God that this song, which came out of our experience in the refugee camps, could be so recognized and so blessed. It was amazing to us. We wrote it knowing nothing at all about the North American music industry. It was the first song we ever wrote in English."

Just attending the Maja Awards gala was an incredible thrill for the brothers.

"This was our first big awards event," Fabian says, "and we were very nervous. It was a fancy red carpet affair with many of the major artists present.

They picked us up from home in a limousine."

The boys knew they had been nominated in the six different categories, but they knew nothing beyond that. Therefore, it came as something of a shock to be asked to perform on stage at the gala.

"A lot of people are saying good things about you," organizers told them. "Your music is playing in Buffalo and New York and we're hearing many good comments on this side of the border, too. We'd like you to perform."

The brothers looked at one another. "We've never done anything like this before," they reminded one another. "We've never walked on the red carpet. The media will be there....We will be way too nervous to sing."

The media was definitely there. The moment Krystaal stepped out of the limousine, cameras began flashing and reporters came running, shoving microphones in their faces and asking, "How do you feel receiving this many awards?"

"We felt like Hollywood stars," Michel says. "I thought: Is this me or someone else? In the waiting room backstage there were all these artists whose faces we recognized from television and videos. We had never been in such company before. Miss Canada presented our trophies."

When Krystaal walked out on the stage after winning the multiple awards, they could hardly hear themselves above the din of the audience shouting, "Krystaal, Krystaal, Krystaal!" They began singing their award-winning song "Keep on Standing," and the response was deafening. People lined up afterward to have photos taken with the brothers from Zaire and get their autographs. The next morning, a Toronto newspaper announced: "Krystaal Sweeps Awards."

Later in the year, the group won two Covenant Awards for Song of the Year and Urban Song of the Year at the Canadian Gospel Music Awards.

"That was a big deal," Michel says. "We were on the platform and could see ourselves on the big screen, while everybody was screaming and shouting, 'Krystaal, Krystaal!' For us, the biggest thrill was being on stage with some of the major bands and Juno winners."

But the honours weren't over yet. Krystaal was nominated in five Shai Award categories that same year.

"It was hard to believe," Fabian says. "After a really rough six months when we first got to Toronto, here we were receiving all these awards. It happened so fast we could hardly keep up. And when people heard we had a book and a testimony to share, things moved even faster."

While all this was happening, the men continued to travel to the United

States to do concerts. Invitations came from Boston, Minneapolis, Chicago, Texas and beyond. In Chicago, the Lwambas were guests at Trinity United Church, which is pastored by Reverend Dr. Jeremiah A. Wright. The church promotes itself as "unashamedly Black and unapologetically Christian."

In September of 2004, Krystaal returned to Saskatoon to visit Leonie and do a concert at Emmanuel Baptist Church. They took along their awards to share with friends there. Fabian's wife Sabina accompanied them. She was now working with World Vision in the child sponsorship department and Saskatoon was one stop on the cross-country sponsorship tour.

Following the concert, Krystaal flew back to Toronto. When they landed at the airport, they learned they were booked to perform that evening at an event put on by Stephen Lewis, the United Nations special envoy for HIV/AIDS in Africa at the time.

The brothers met Lewis earlier in the year when they performed with some other World Vision contracted artists at a gala $500-a-plate fundraiser dinner. Stephen Lewis was there, speaking on behalf of children in Africa with HIV/AIDS.

The brothers barely had time to get home, drop off their luggage and head out to the event. They took along the trophies.

"We had no idea how big the event would be," Fabian says ruefully. "My wife was still on the World Vision sponsorship tour and I didn't have time to find a babysitter, so I brought along Gill and little Joellyn and then had to ask someone to keep an eye on them while we sang. As well, we figured it would be an informal gathering, so we didn't bother to change our clothes. As it turned out, it was a huge gala with 1,000 people in attendance, including the mayor of Toronto. Everyone else was in formal attire. We showed up in jeans and we have the pictures to prove it. I have always regretted that. We were assigned to the head table. There we were, Michel, Aliston and me dressed in blue jeans, sitting with Stephen Lewis and the mayor of Toronto."

Yet the crowd loved their music. They loved it even more when Krystaal showed them the trophies. Taking one, Stephen Lewis held it high. "I have been to Kisangani, Congo," he told the audience. "I have been to their land and I know what they came through. I just want you to know I am very happy to be working with these men."

On Boxing Day of 2004, the Lwambas, along with all the rest of the world, were shocked and saddened to hear of the devastation wreaked on southeast Asia by the December 26 tsunami. Ironically, that same tsunami would have a positive impact on their lives, but it was also a chilling picture of the devastation they themselves would experience in the upcoming year.

Chapter Fourteen

THROUGH A THOROUGHLY CIRCUITOUS CHAIN OF EVENTS, THE SAME TSUNAMI that brought tragedy and destruction to southeast Asia opened an important door of opportunity for Krystaal.

When the Canada for Asia Tsunami Relief concert was being organized to air on CBC Television, a Christian rap artist from Winnipeg, Fresh I.E., was invited to be part of the program.

Fresh I.E. (aka Rob Wilson) is a recording artist and a youth leader at an inner-city ministry in Winnipeg called Living Bible Explorers. Not only was Fresh the first Gospel music artist to be nominated for a Grammy award, he has been nominated for that honour twice.

Krystaal met Fresh I.E. at the 2004 Shai Awards, Canada's Gospel music version of the People's Choice Awards, where both he and Krystaal had nominations. At the awards, the four talked about the possibility of performing together some day. Krystaal had a song they had written called "Stay On The Way" that they felt would benefit from the input of a rapper like Fresh.

It was Fresh I.E. who invited Krystaal to back up his performance at the Canada for Asia event. They performed a song Fresh wrote specifically for the concert that aired on January 13, 2005.

The men heard about the invitation via cell phone as they were flying home from a concert in Atlanta, Georgia. They were stunned to learn they would be on stage with stars like Bryan Adams, Rush, Blue Rodeo, Jann Arden, Oscar

Peterson, Anne Murray and more. Everything was set; the arrangements were made; all they had to do was show up.

It was an unbelievable experience. Here were three boys from the refugee camp standing beside celebrities like Wayne Gretzky, Céline Dion, Don Cherry and Bryan Adams, whom Michel had admired since childhood. Now he was meeting Adams in person and being complimented by him.

Others, too, were impressed by Krystaal's performance. Anne Murray wanted an autograph from Michel. He was absorbed in conversation with someone else when she stepped up and he didn't recognize her right away. But Fabian did. He was unashamedly star struck.

"I consider Anne Murray to be the First Lady of Canadian music," he says. "The first year I came to Canada, I saw Anne Murray's face on a Christmas CD advertised on television. Now here I was, face to face with her. I said, 'You're Anne Murray.'"

"Yes," she said. "Come here, boys. Let's take a picture."

Krystaal was also photographed with Canadian novelist Margaret Atwood, after approaching her for an autograph. Atwood was talking to legendary pianist Oscar Peterson who said, "Come here, boys. Let's have a picture."

World Vision executive director Dave Toycen would later tell Krystaal that a million dollars' worth of donations were phoned in immediately following their performance with Fresh I.E. The news was thrilling and humbling at the same time.

In mid-January, 2005, Krystaal packed their bags and equipment and flew to Tanzania. Not long before, the family had learned their sister Cecile was alive and living in a refugee camp in Arusha, Tanzania, with her children.

Cecile was special within the family. She was Gilbert Lwamba's favourite daughter and the brothers remember how, many times, their father cancelled important meetings to go and visit her.

Cecile received her education in Bukavu in eastern Zaire and it was there that she met and married television journalist Mesombuko Saidi Zamarudi. From the very beginning, Gilbert was concerned about the marriage because Zamarudi was part Rwandan. He consented to the union, but his concern remained high. He visited often to make sure his daughter was happy and living comfortably.

Things seemed to be going well. Cecile and her husband had five children. Zamarudi's career was flourishing. He was promoted to an office on the fifth floor of the Voice of Zaire media building in downtown Bukavu.

Beneath the surface, however, trouble was brewing. Mobutu's government was increasingly unhappy that someone of "mixed blood" was occupying such an influential position. Matters came to a head when Zamarudi made the comment on national television that all Congolese should be equal, even those with Rwandan blood. Shortly after, Zamarudi was accosted by Mobutu's thugs and thrown out his fifth floor office window.

Cecile was summoned to the office, ostensibly to see her husband. What she saw was her husband's body splattered all over the pavement in front of the building. His murderers forced her to collect the pieces. The message was blatant: "If you or anyone else in your family meddles in Zairean politics, you will all end up like this."

Shattered and terrified by the episode, Cecile returned to her home to find the lovely house burned to the ground. She knew then and there there would be more slaughter if the extremists found her mixed-blood children—a 16-year-old son and 4 beautiful daughters. She knew they would all be exterminated if they didn't leave Zaire immediately.

Cecile and her children slipped across the border into Rwanda. Being part Rwandan, Cecile thought surely her children would be accepted and safe there. But the situation was no better.

"We don't want you here," Rwandan authorities told Cecile. "You are Congolese."

When they saw her young son, they immediately wanted to put him in the army. Cecile resisted. She knew with his Congolese blood he would be cannon fodder. Because he was neither full-blooded Congolese nor full-blooded Rwandan, he would be relegated to the front lines where he was sure to be killed.

Since there was no place for them in Rwanda, Cecile took her children across the eastern border into Tanzania. The family ended up in a refugee camp in Arusha.

Michel and Fabian arrived in Tanzania in January of 2005 and sent word to Cecile that they were on their way to Arusha. When she received the message, Cecile fainted. She had given up the hope of ever seeing her brothers again. So many years had passed since Fabian lived in Cecile's home in Bukavu while he attended high school. In fact, the last time he saw Cecile's son, the boy was a baby crawling on the floor. Now he was a young man.

For the brothers, seeing Cecile again after all those years was a shock. She had gone through so many traumas and had physically changed so much that they hardly recognized her. Cecile was still suffering from intense psychological trauma and had a serious heart condition, as well. Fabian found himself thinking over and over again, "If Dad could see her now, how he would weep."

The abysmal state in which they found Cecile and her children living brought back vivid memories of the refugee camps. Having now spent several years in Canada, they had forgotten much of the horrendous conditions of the camps. The brothers thanked God all over again for rescuing them.

Now they had to figure out a way to rescue their sister.

First, Fabian and Michel took Cecile to a doctor to get medication for her heart condition.

The boys cried when they saw how their sister and her children were living and what they were eating. The six of them slept in a little cubbyhole no bigger than the average clothes closet.

They cried even more when Cecile told them her story. "We thought we went through a lot," Fabian says, shaking his head sadly, "but it was nothing compared to Cecile's experience and how she and her children were treated in the camp."

Through sobs and tears, Cecile described her husband's death. She handed Michel a videotape with filmed footage of her husband's mangled body on the ground. It was a gift from Mobutu's people. Michel could never bring himself to watch it.

Michel and Fabian grieved with Cecile and comforted her as best they could. Then they set about moving the little family to Kenya to await immigration processing to Canada. The news that Peoples Church in Toronto would sponsor them through World Vision moved Cecile to tears again. This time her tears were tinged with hope—something she had not experienced in years.

The Lwamba brothers had another reason for being in Arusha. Their visit coincided with a two-week ministry crusade for Krystaal with Christopher Mwakasege, a teacher, preacher, economist and advisor to the Government of Tanzania.

"We met Pastor Christopher in Boston when he came to one of our concerts," Michel says. "He said, 'I like what you're doing with your music ministry and your message of reconciliation. We should put together a crusade in Arusha.' We told him we were planning to go to Tanzania to look for our sister and he immediately set to work organizing a crusade to coincide with our visit."

The crusade became a "Peace Tour," a concept God had been stirring in Krystaal's heart. More and more, the men were feeling that God wanted to use the pain and hardship they had endured and the forgiveness and reconciliation they experienced to help others. The Arusha crusade would be a test case to see if they were hearing correctly and if peace tours were indeed where God wanted their music ministry to go.

For 15 days, Krystaal provided the praise and worship music and Christopher Mwakasege preached. Together, they encouraged the people to settle their differences and, through the power of Jesus Christ, to forgive one another.

Average attendance for the 15 days was staggering: 124,000 per day, with 1,500 ushers controlling the crowd. The weather was windy and rainy, but no one seemed to care. People began arriving at 11 a.m., even though the event didn't start until late afternoon. When Krystaal showed up at 3 p.m. to do sound checks, there were already 20,000 to 30,000 people assembled and waiting.

The crusade was supposed to be an indoor event, but when it became evident the building reserved would not begin to hold everybody, the city offered its outdoor sports field. A big tent was erected for the people on stage, but the audience was outside, most of them sitting on the ground.

Because of the time spent getting Cecile settled in Kenya, Krystaal arrived at the crusade two days late. They couldn't believe the size of the crowds that had already been coming for two days.

"When we walked onto the stage, we just stood there with our mouths open," Michel recalls. "We had never seen so many people in an audience before. The stage was in the middle and when you looked out over the crowd, you couldn't see the end of it in any direction. There were so many people, the speaker system couldn't carry the sound to everyone. All the buses in Arusha were directed to this site. Shops in the city were closed. That's how much of an impact those meetings had."

People came for the music and the message. Many came to see Krystaal just because they were from Canada. Some had seen the group on "100 Huntley Street," which is broadcast on Tanzanian television. Others had seen their music video "Stay on the Way" played on local television stations. For them, the three Congolese-Canadians were already music icons.

Krystaal started the meetings with songs of praise to God. Then they stopped for a time of prayer before moving into worship music. They sang for two hours straight, then Pastor Christopher preached his message of peace, forgiveness and reconciliation.

"These people were hungry for peace," Fabian says. "The United Nations and other agencies are trying their best to bring peace to Africa, but nothing is working. We know the only lasting and real peace comes from the Prince of Peace who brings light to a dark world and changes people from the inside out. We know that from personal experience because we lived in the dark. We learned that the only way to move on with our lives after all that happened is to let the past go. And the only way to do that is through the power of Christ."

Christopher Mwakasege's messages were powerful. His words cut through the hatred and tension. There were people in the crowd who hadn't spoken to one another in years. There were people from many different tribes, people divided by ancient and not-so-ancient conflicts. Arusha was where the war crimes tribunals for the Rwandan genocide were being held, so there were many Rwandans present—Hutus who perpetrated the genocide and Tutsi survivors. There were Congolese who had experienced devastating losses. And there were many Tanzanians with their own problems.

"Do you want to find healing and forgiveness from the things that have happened in your life?" Christopher Mwakasege challenged. "If you want to find the freedom to get on with your life, do it right now. Come for prayer. Come to worship Jesus Christ. How many want to let the past go?"

People literally ran to the front screaming and crying. Thousands came, even young children. Day after day, the brothers couldn't believe the response.

After 15 days of ministering, the Peace Tour was over. On the last day, Krystaal told the audience they would be leaving and going back to Canada. When they arrived at the venue the next morning to dismantle the stage and pack up their equipment, they found 10,000 or so people already there waiting, begging them to sing some more, wanting to hear them speak.

"If that can happen in Tanzania, it can happen anywhere in the world," Michel observes. "It can happen in Canada and the United States, too. And what about Congo, where we come from?

"Today, the Church in Africa is playing a bigger role in people's lives than politicians are. If the Church is willing to spread the teaching of forgiveness, hope and reconciliation, I believe it will have more impact than any legislated measures, especially in places like Congo and central Africa. People go to a church there and worship, but because of old tribal conflicts, they won't sit together. I don't think the Church even thinks of this as an issue and as a result, Africa keeps going down.

"We want to create opportunities for people to come face to face with peace and reconciliation. Music is a powerful tool that can bring people together. It is a universal language that everyone can understand. We truly believe God wants to use our experiences, our story and our music to bring peace and healing."

The experience in Arusha made the brothers take a fresh look at the gift of peace and forgiveness they now enjoyed. "You have to come to the place where you know you can't find peace unless you have Jesus Christ in your heart," Fabian says. "Peace and forgiveness is between man and man, but first, it has to be between God and man. You must first reconcile with God. There's no way we can love each other if we don't love God."

That truth would soon be put to the test in their own lives.

Since moving to Toronto, Krystaal had been working hard to put their faces and their unique music in the public's eye. That meant accepting any and every invitation that came along to perform and grasping any opportunity that would advance them in the professional music industry.

In order to be competitive in the industry and raise their profile nationally and internationally, the boys felt Krystaal needed to make a music video. So when a producer sought them out and offered to make a video for them, it seemed like a smart thing to do.

The person who approached them boasted all the right credentials. He said he was an experienced video director with connections to Mel Gibson's Icon Company and that he had worked on the filming of "The Passion of the Christ," a blockbuster hit at the time.

The director's initial proposal was to make a documentary of the Lwamba brothers' life story, but that was not a direction in which they wanted to go.

"If you want to do something with us, you can do a music video," Michel told him.

"I'll do better than that. I'll help you do three videos," the producer countered. "And because I like you guys, I'll give you a break. You're well aware that it can cost as much as $100,000 to make one video. I'll do three for you for $14,000. I can give you a deal because I already have all the equipment and the people in place."

The bargain was too good to pass up. The men scraped together every dollar they could find, including the money the family had been putting aside to buy a house. They handed over the $14,000.

The first video was a three-minute production of Krystaal's song "Stay On The Way," which they planned to release with a new CD that was almost complete.

The video production was quite an undertaking. Shooting venues were identified and leased, a Hummer and a helicopter were rented, actors were engaged and technicians were hired, including John Petrella, a professional cameraman who had worked on numerous successful documentaries and films.

Partway through the shooting, Petrella called Michel and Fabian aside. "This producer guy doesn't know what he's doing," he said. "I've worked with major movie and video directors and he isn't one. I think he's a fake. Get rid of him now and I'll help you guys finish this project."

The brothers were in a quandary. As they took a step backward to review the project, they realized that what Petrella said was true. They fired the so-called producer and turned the project over to the veteran cameraman. At least they would get one video done.

But the worst was yet to come.

At the end of shooting, all the technicians, actors and rental agencies presented their bills to Krystaal Inc. The Lwambas were stunned. Their understanding was that the $14,000 they paid up front would cover all the expenses. In truth, all that was covered was the lining of the so-called producer's pocket.

The bills were staggering. There was the lighting company to pay and the sound people. There were invoices for actors, props and the rental of the helicopter and the Hummer. The bill for a few hours' use of one location alone was $7,000. In total, the tab came to over $50,000.

There was no way Krystaal could pay their creditors. Their bank accounts were drained; their credit cards were maxed out. The only thing they could do was promise payment as soon as they were able.

The debt was crippling. Every dollar they made at concerts for the next many months went to pay off the creditors. It was only Betty's and Sabina's jobs that kept a roof over their heads and food on the table.

Michel, especially, was devastated. Not only was their money gone, so was their band. They had pulled together a fine instrumental ensemble to back up their concerts. Now the musicians had moved on to other things because Krystaal couldn't afford to pay them. Michel understood and wished them all the best. Like him, they had families to feed and support.

The fact that they had been taken in by a shyster was a bitter pill for the boys to swallow. "We learned the hard way that not everyone is reputable and trustworthy," Fabian reflects. "I guess we were spoiled by all those years on the Prairies where people are basically more honest."

Even harder was finding genuine forgiveness for the man who cheated them.

The experience forced Krystaal to re-evaluate their lives and everything they were doing.

"We got lost in the business," Michel admits. "We were so busy trying to 'make it' in the music industry, that our time with God was suffering. Oh, we were praying for His help and His blessing, but our time was at a premium. God had to let us get into this impossible situation to remind us that we were neglecting the most important thing of all—spending time with Him and seeking His face. That is more important than our career, our ministry or our place in the music industry."

Once more the brothers devoted themselves to prayer. One of their requests was that they would find a way to deal with the critical financial situation.

The answer came in the form of many more invitations to perform. If the men thought they were busy before, now they could hardly keep up. Some of the invitations came in the most unusual ways, like one pastor who happened upon their website and invited them to come and do a concert in his church.

Every dollar the men made went to pay down the bills.

"This whole thing made us realize that God cares about us even when we make mistakes," Fabian says. "He is a God of mercy. No matter how hard it is, when you come back to God, He will show you a way through it."

When the "Stay on the Way" video was finally released, it won Favourite Video of the Year at the 2006 Maja Awards. Krystaal's song of the same name was released as a single and was nominated for Urban Song of the Year at the 2006 Canadian Gospel Music Awards.

Immediately after the filming of the video, Krystaal went to Texas to perform at a conference. Fabian took Sabina and his children with him; Michel took his daughter Denise.

"It was Sabina's birthday," Fabian says. "I wanted her to have something special to say thank you for the wonderful support she has always been to me. Both she and Betty were so strong during the video episode. We've seen them devastated over little things, but in this case, they never wavered. They were consistently encouraging, even though we lost all the money that was supposed to buy a home for us.

"We can't say enough about the support we receive from Betty and Sabina. They are tremendous spouses. After all they've been through in their lives, it wasn't easy on them or the kids to move from the loving community we had in Saskatoon to Toronto. It was hard for everyone to re-adjust. At the beginning, we all lived together in one townhouse. It is hard enough for brothers to share one house, let alone two women. But those ladies ran the house together and handled themselves so well. When it came time for Sabina and I to move into our own place, it was hard to say goodbye."

The Texas engagement was followed by a trip to Milton Keynes, England, for a performance and then on to the Jesus Celebration Centre Conference in Scarborough, England. This was their first visit to Great Britain and it came at the invitation of Pastor Wilfred Lai, who operates a centre to train African church leaders. Lai had heard Krystaal in North America and read their book. He invited the group to perform at an annual Jesus Celebration that draws Christians from all over England. At least 6,000 gathered to hear Krystaal in Scarborough. Later, they went to Liverpool to participate in an event put on by Easter People, an association of churches in the Liverpool area.

After each gig and concert tour, the men came back home and paid the bills.

The time was fast approaching for Krystaal to return to England for the World Baptist Congress in Birmingham, England. This would be their highest profile performance opportunity yet. They arranged to preface the time in Birmingham with a concert tour to France and Belgium, but there was something they had to do first.

Upon relocating to Toronto, Krystaal rented space in a business building on Front Street in downtown Toronto and built themselves a studio, where they practised and did recording work. One of their projects was a new CD.

They had been working on this new CD prior to the move to Toronto. It was a beautiful album, full of original material, all songs they had written. One they particularly liked was an Easter song. The CD was now about 99% finished. All 12 tracks were recorded and preserved on computer files. The only thing that remained was to add vocals to a couple of the songs.

The brothers went to great lengths and considerable expense to make this album as professional as possible, even hiring additional musicians and renting appropriate locations in which to record certain instruments. Every moment they weren't performing, they were working in the studio. The album was entitled "Solid Faith," and Krystaal planned to launch it in the fall of 2005.

Now they were once again forced to suspend work on the CD because the owner of the building where their studio was located sold the building. Krystaal Inc. had to move.

With their busy performance schedule and the upcoming tour to Belgium and England, there wasn't a lot of time to look for new digs and make a leisurely move. The best they could do was remove the equipment and deal with the rest of it when they returned.

In the process of packing up the equipment, the unthinkable happened. The computer file with the recorded music for the new CD was lost.

In the blink of an eye or the inadvertent flick of a finger, months and months of hard work was erased.

Chapter Fifteen

COMING SO HARD ON THE HEELS OF THE VIDEO FIASCO AND THE CRIPPLING debt load Krystaal was still carrying, the loss of the CD seemed to be more than they could handle.

Fabian still shakes his head at the memory. "I don't know how it happened," he says. "I don't know what I did. It's one of those things that can happen with computers. Somehow the file went into the computer garbage bin and I erased the garbage. I watched it disappear. I said, 'Please, no, this can't be happening.'"

The brothers made frantic phone calls to a number of computer recovery services. "Oh, yes," the companies said, "we can retrieve your data. We have recovered lost tsunami donation files and bank files. We can recover yours." But, in the end, no one could find any trace of the deleted music file.

Michel, Fabian and Aliston were devastated. Not only had they lost tens of thousands of dollars on a bad video deal, now their entire CD was gone. It was too bizarre to be coincidental.

Maybe, they thought, this was a message. Maybe they weren't meant to continue in ministry. Perhaps it was time to stop. Surely, if they were doing what God wanted, all of this would not be happening to them.

The brothers were thoroughly discouraged. Things were so bad, they began to talk seriously about quitting.

A couple of things persuaded them to carry on. One was a phone call that came from a pastor in Washington, D.C., someone they had never met before.

"God has shown me that you men are going through a difficult time," the pastor said. "I'm just calling to tell you to hang in there. Don't give up. God is preparing something big for you."

A second call came from a man in England, a man they knew as Pastor Al. Pastor Al said, "God revealed to me that you are going through something very discouraging right now. I don't know what it is, but I'm praying for you. I believe God is preparing you for a significant ministry in the future."

The third factor was the commitments Krystaal had already made to tour France and Belgium and afterward, to perform at the Baptist World Congress in Birmingham, England. As best they could, they put aside their discouragement and prepared for the upcoming European tour.

It began in Paris, then went on to Liège, Belgium, and ended up in Maline near Brussels. In Maline, they were part of an outdoor youth rally at a train station. The day was a civic holiday and there were streams of people coming and going to the train station. All of them heard the music and many stopped to listen and hear what Krystaal had to say.

In ministering to their European audiences, the brothers also ministered to themselves. "It was all very powerful and very emotional," Fabian says, "and it helped us regain our perspective and focus on our ministry again instead of being lost in the business end of things."

It was in Belgium one night that Aliston had an unusual dream. He dreamed he saw God working alongside Krystaal, helping a large crowd of children move toward a door. Krystaal was urging the children to go through the doorway to join a celebration of some kind that was happening on the other side. In the dream, Aliston and his brothers were shaking people who were asleep, trying to wake them up so they wouldn't miss the party.

In the morning, he told his brothers about the dream. "I don't know what it means," he said, "but I think it means something good."

With somewhat lighter hearts, Krystaal left Europe and flew to Birmingham, England.

Cal Malena and Gary Nelson, the general secretary of Canadian Baptist Ministries, had submitted Krystaal's name and samples of their music to the organizing committee of the Baptist World Congress, which was convening in Birmingham in July of 2005 to celebrate its 100th anniversary.

The Baptist World Alliance is a global fellowship of about 80 million Baptists in 214 national unions or conventions in 200 countries of the world. Every five years, the BWA holds an international gathering or congress, which draws about 15,000 delegates of all Baptist stripes from around the world. Christian artists, bands and choirs from the various participating countries are invited to perform and lead praise and worship at the conference. Krystaal was one of the bands selected for the 2005 congress.

Krystaal had no idea what to expect. They checked out the BWA website, but the information there conveyed little of the enormity of the event or its ministry potential.

Upon arriving in Birmingham, the brothers were taken to the local Symphony Hall where they would perform with all the other groups in a gala music concert. They were stunned by the size and beauty of the place, and awed to realize that this was the venue used when the Queen was in attendance.

From there, they went to view the city's big soccer arena, the National Indoor Arena. That, too, was huge. It would be the site of a number of outdoor concerts throughout the week.

There were several opportunities at the congress for Krystaal to perform and minister. One was in Symphony Hall, where each artist and group performed a short program. There were large gatherings at the arena in the evenings and a Highlight Night to end the congress. During the day, delegates could choose which praise and worship session they wanted to attend. Many came again and again to hear Krystaal.

Each day a different continent was highlighted. There was European Day, African Day and Asian Day, where a 150-voice choir from South Korea head-lined. Krystaal thought it rather amusing that they were part of North American Day. The brothers found themselves on stage with an American song leader, a church choir from Beaufort, South Carolina, Rev. Rick Warren (pastor of Saddleback Church in Southern California and author of "The Purpose Driven Life") and former United States President Jimmy Carter.

The event organizers hadn't planned to have Krystaal headline on the stage that day. They had another group in mind, but after hearing the Lwambas at one of the outdoor concerts, they changed their minds.

As the North American contingent was lining up and waiting to go on stage, President Jimmy Carter was in front of Michel, Fabian and Aliston and Rick Warren was behind them. They had already become acquainted and Michel gave both men a copy of *Keep on Standing*. Now, as they waited, Michel pinched Fabian's arm. "Is this really us?" he whispered. "Are these guys standing with President Jimmy Carter and Rev. Rick Warren the same ones who were in a refugee camp not so long ago?"

Then it was time to go on stage.

As they walked to the front of the platform to sing, thousands of voices began shouting, "Krystaal! Krystaal! Krystaal!" The Canadian contingent in the audience, which included Cal and Joanne Malena and Gary Nelson, waved their Canadian flags wildly.

"We felt so proud to be Canadians," Fabian says, his voice choked with emotion at the memory. "It was our proudest moment."

Fabian, who functions as the spokesperson for Krystaal, began by telling the audience how proud and happy Krystaal was to be working with Canadian Baptist Ministries, reaching lives around the globe and going to the very difficult areas of the world to make a difference. Then the brothers sang a number of songs including "I Must Have Jesus" and "He's a Miracle-Working God." The audience loved them and wanted more.

After they left the stage, Fabian pulled Michel off to one side. The two stood together and wept. "We were stunned by the experience and deeply moved that God would bring the three of us out of the refugee camp to this," Fabian says. "We never for one second thought we would ever have such a thrilling and inspiring experience. 'Do you remember where we came from?' I asked Michel. 'We were living in those little tents.'"

The two grasped hands and with tears streaming down their faces, they praised and thanked God. "Only You could bring about something as wonderful as this," they said.

When the service ended, the brothers were thronged by people who wanted to meet the members of Krystaal personally, buy their book and CDs and get their autographs. One individual who came to speak to them was Pastor Al, who had called several weeks before to encourage them. Again he told them, "God is preparing something big for you."

The response to Krystaal at the Baptist World Congress was astonishing. It was so tremendous that David Coffey, president of the Baptist World Alliance, called the worship experience "unprecedented." According to a Birmingham book store, Krystaal sold more product than any other group at the conference. They were also popular guests on a television talk show format that aired each day. Many who heard the interviews wanted to know more about these three men and read their story.

A number of interesting opportunities came out of the congress. Krystaal was immediately booked for the 2010 BWA Congress in Hawaii and the Baptist Youth World Conference in Leipzig, Germany, in 2008. As well, they were invited to lead worship at a British Baptist Alliance conference in England. Rick Warren issued an invitation for Krystaal to minister at Saddleback Church and another invitation came from Rev. Billy Kim, former president of the Baptist World Alliance and pastor of the 15,000 member Suwon Central Baptist Church in Seoul, Korea.

The Korean invitation came rather inauspiciously.

After the service, as Michel was signing autographs for enthusiastic fans, he noticed a well-dressed Asian man who seemed to be following him.

"Can I help you?" Michel asked.

The man indicated he would like Michel's business card.

Michel quickly searched through his pockets. "I've run out of cards," he said. "So many people wanted one. But if you will wait right here, I'll go and get you a card."

The man nodded.

Unfortunately, Michel got waylaid several times by fans and admirers and it was some time before he got back to the Asian man. In the meantime, the gentleman had purchased Krystaal's book.

Michel handed the man his card and accepted one in return. With a smile and a nod, he slipped the card in his pocket and moved on to the next person asking for an autograph.

Someone grasped his arm and asked, "Do you know who that man is?"

"No," Michel admitted.

"He's the vice-president of South Korea."

Michel quickly pulled out the card. His jaw dropped when he read it. He had just put the vice-president of South Korea on hold!

Michel pushed through the crowd and caught up with the vice-president, who was moving within his ring of bodyguards. "I am so sorry," he exclaimed. "Please forgive me. I didn't mean to ignore you."

The gracious man explained that he was hereby inviting Krystaal to South Korea for a concert tour. "When you come," he said, "you will be under my care."

The vice-president went on to say that his pastor, Dr. Billy Kim, would be getting in touch with Krystaal to make the arrangements. He added that while Kim's church was a relatively small one, with only 18,000 members, there were many other churches in Korea that would be eager to host Krystaal's ministry.

Michel later learned that the vice-president is an usher in Pastor Kim's church and the person who prevailed out of several who wanted to underwrite the cost of tickets for the 150-voice Korean choir to travel to the congress.

The entire experience in Birmingham was tremendously affirming for the Lwamba brothers. At the same time, it was humbling. They had come with doubts about whether they should continue in ministry; they left with full reassurance that God was still interested in using their music, their songs and their story to touch people's hearts and change their lives.

Upon returning to Toronto, Krystaal received the news that a special fan of theirs had died in their absence. The fan was a woman who first heard their song "Keep on Standing" on the radio as she lay in her hospital bed undergoing cancer treatment. It happened shortly after the song had won multiple awards at the Maja Awards.

The woman was so impacted by the words of "Keep on Standing" that she immediately called the station to ask where she could get a copy of the CD. The disc jockey was unable to make contact with the Lwambas and personally drove to the hospital to give the woman a CD.

The lady played the disc continuously and found great comfort in the words of "Keep on Standing." Even more important, she became personally acquainted with the God and Saviour that Krystaal sang about in the song.

After a brief recovery period, the woman suffered a relapse. When she realized her cancer was terminal, she put the song on repeat. She died listening to "Keep on Standing." Her final request was that Krystaal be at her funeral, but because they were away in Birmingham, a Maja Award representative went on their behalf.

Hearing the story was tremendously moving and it was another confirmation to the men that God was still at work in their ministry and their music.

Coming back to Canada brought the Lwambas back to rude reality. Yet, somehow, their perspective on things had changed. They were able to look at their situation more objectively. Yes, they had lost a CD; no, they didn't have a studio, but the debts were slowly diminishing and invitations continued to pour in. The brothers felt it was a good time to stand still and examine where they had been and where they were going.

Where they had been was somewhere far too busy. "We were so busy, we didn't have time to pray," Michel confesses. "Because of it, we were missing something absolutely essential—quality time with God. The more we thought about it, the more we began to wonder if the video fiasco and losing our CD was God's way of stopping the treadmill we were on and bringing us to our knees in prayer.

"We also realized that we were heading in a direction of our own choosing, trying to produce music that pleased the industry, when all along, God wanted us to please Him. It was very sobering to recognize that. We saw that we needed to reconnect with God. We needed to stop working so frantically and simply seek God's face. From that moment on, we committed ourselves to spending a lot of time in prayer."

The lost CD was still a painful recollection that none of the brothers wanted to think about, but the memory gradually faded as the inspiration for a new album began to grow. This one would be a praise and worship album. They knew the idea came straight from the heart of God and that He would use it to touch many people.

"The CD we lost was very industry oriented," Fabian observes in retrospect. "We were trying so hard to do everything according to what we thought the industry and the secular market wanted. That had become our focus, even though our primary aim was still always to offer praise and worship to God and to deepen our relationship with Him. But somewhere along the line, that all got mixed up with the business part. We were too busy building our studio, shooting our video and working on our album, to stop and figure out what God wanted.

"Producers would tell us, 'This praise and worship song of yours is not going to appeal to the general media,' so we began writing nice catchy lines and good melodies that we figured would appeal to both secular and Christian radio stations. We wanted to fit in with both sides of the industry. The problem is, when you start squelching the things that are most important to your faith, you are basically saying, 'God has done marvellous things for us in the past, but we can handle it now.'"

With new insight and fresh inspiration, Krystaal returned to Belgium for a youth convention in the fall of 2005, then went to Kenya to sing at a Jesus Celebration Centre convention in Mombasa stadium. Attendance was estimated at 70,000.

The year ended with another trip to England and a large concert on New Year's Eve at New Wine Church in London. The attendance was 9,000. In between, there were concert trips in Canada and the US. One was the 10th anniversary of the Assembly of the Lutheran World Federation which was held in Winnipeg, Manitoba, and drew 40,000 Lutherans from 81 countries of the world.

A particularly gratifying gig was a two-week concert tour in Beaufort, South Carolina.

It began when Rev. Dr. Harry Rowland, pastor of the Baptist Church of Beaufort, and his wife Lana were delegates to the Baptist World Congress in Birmingham. There they heard Krystaal in concert and were immediately drawn to the brothers' story and ministry. They believed that Krystaal embodied what it meant to be missional Christians, the theme of a renewal weekend Rowland's church was planning for January, 2006.

Following the congress, the Rowlands and 13 other delegates from South Carolina continued on to Belgium, where some worked on a church construction project near Ostend and the rest participated in a prayer ministry among Belgium Baptist Union pastors and leaders. It was there that the Rowland's connected with Patrick and Ria Deneut.

The conversation soon came around to Krystaal. Harry expressed the wish that he could have the men come to his church for the upcoming Renewal Weekend.

"Would you like to get in touch with them?" Patrick inquired.

"I would. Do you know them?"

Patrick grinned. "I know them well. They call me their uncle. It's our little joke."

The ensuing visit to Beaufort turned out to be more than just a series of concert performances for Krystaal. Through the foresight of Harry Rowland, the brothers were able to bring a powerful ministry of healing and reconciliation to the beautiful American city, with its long connection to slavery.

Lana Rowland took Michel, Fabian and Aliston on a tour of the historic town and pointed out where the slave ships used to land and the square where the slave auctions took place.

"You can just sense that something of consequence happened there," Fabian says.

Harry Rowland arranged for Krystaal to sing and speak at a number of school assemblies during their two weeks in Beaufort. In the high school, especially, students were drawn to the music and the brothers' stories of life in the refugee camp. They identified with Aliston, who was exactly their age when he was in the camp.

"Why would you come to Beaufort when you've been all over the world?" one student asked.

"Because Beaufort is a place in this world and it is a place where we have Christian brothers and sisters," Fabian replied. "Therefore, it is a place where we want to share our ministry of reconciliation, which is for everyone everywhere."

Rowland, too, felt that Krystaal's message of reconciliation could be important for his city and church. His congregation was working intentionally to bridge the gap between the wealthy residential community of Beaufort and the disadvantaged African American sector.

"Krystaal was the first Black group ever to lead a week-long event in the Baptist Church of Beaufort," Rowland reports, "and they were the first Black people our congregation ever hosted and lived with. It gave them a chance to realize what reconciliation and love really are as they heard the stories of the refugee camp and connected them with the gentle, peaceful and gracious lives of Krystaal."

The powerfully positive experience in Beaufort laid the foundation for the Lwambas' return to Toronto to begin work on the new praise and worship album. They titled it "Speak to Me." Fabian wrote some new songs, arranged the music and directed and produced the CD himself.

After the video fiasco, the brothers were determined to let as little of their work as possible leave their hands. That included recording and producing their music.

The brothers outfitted another recording studio that soon became a house of production. They called their media company "Braveman Studios." (The African word for "braveman" is *lwamba*.)

Krystaal Inc. invested in good equipment and software that would enable them to record and produce music CDs and videos for themselves and for other artists. Fabian entered into a mentorship program with a recording industry professional and began taking university level classes in multimedia studies.

"We didn't want to listen to advice from other producers about how this album should be made," Fabian says. "We wanted to do it the way we believed God was putting into our hearts to make it."

"When we started to do "Speak to Me," we almost began going in the same direction as before," Michel says. "Fortunately, we stopped in our tracks and said, 'God, we want You to direct us.' We started to praise God a little more and worship Him while we were recording in the studio. I remember during one song, we just stopped in the middle of recording and began worshipping God. We had never done that with any other album. I believe we connected with God a little deeper."

With the exception of guest instrumentalists on two of the tracks, the "Speak to Me" CD was backed exclusively by singers from the Lwamba family, including George and the children. Fabian credits Edwine, who led worship at

George's Montréal church and "did an amazing job of turning the Lwamba children into singers."

Whenever possible, Sakina, Edwine and George's oldest daughter, Nicole, sing backup at Krystaal concerts. They also perform as an a cappella group, JC (Jesus Christ) Angels.

"Speak to Me" was released in March, 2006. It generated more interest than anything else that Krystaal had done to that point.

"We learned a lot of things from our loss and our 'down in the depths' experience," Fabian muses aloud. "One of the things we learned is the importance of tithing. It is essential for Christians to be good stewards for the sake of the Gospel. We have learned to partner with other ministries—not just with what Krystaal does. That, too, has been a blessing.

"We have also learned to be good partners in business. Having something terrible happen to you makes you want to do everything in your power to prevent a similar thing from happening to someone else."

While all of that is important, Michel, Fabian and Aliston consider the greatest thing to have come out of their difficulties to be the recommitment of their lives and music to God.

"We aren't doing music just for ourselves," Michel says. "It is not about us or about any good music that we play. It is about God's purpose for our lives. He will not allow us to do just anything.

"As our story shows, we have had many ups and downs, but we choose to focus on the ups. A lot of things could have dragged us down—and some did for a while—but we have made the deliberate decision to ignore the negatives and focus on the positive. A person can choose to be happy or sad. We choose to look on the bright side."

In the midst of all of the setbacks, they had sensed God guiding them in a new direction, with a vision for peace tours that would bring a positive message of forgiveness and reconciliation around the world. "Our lesson in forgiveness began in the refugee camp, praying for those who committed crimes against us and our families," Michel explains. "When we tell people how we came to the point of forgiveness, we see them responding. We see people wanting to find that same forgiveness themselves. Forgiveness frees two people and one of them is yourself."

He adds, "Living through the horrible things that happened in our country was not easy, nor was it easy to forgive those responsible. The natural human response is to want revenge and many people from Zaire have come to North

178

America intending to get a good job and make enough money to go back to Zaire and take revenge. We are trying to break that cycle. We have given up the political fight. We are fighting for Jesus now.

"Forgiveness is not human. It is divine. God gave us the ability to forgive. You can only understand forgiveness when you are close to Jesus, who is divine.

"If people want to find peace in this world, let us show them that we have Christ. Let us show them that we have found what it takes to have happiness in this life. Jesus is all we need. He brought peace 2,000 years ago for those who will embrace Him and His life. That is our message, too. You don't have to search all over for peace. It is right here. Jesus Christ is the Peace of the world."

Krystaal's mission for peace and reconciliation has not gone unnoticed. In 2006, they received a Maja Award for being international ambassadors of peace.

In October of the same year, they were honoured at a Planet Africa Awards gala. Planet Africa is a program that celebrates leadership, excellence and professionalism in people of African origin. Krystaal was presented with the Rising Star Award. They stood with other illustrious winners that included physicians, writers, representatives of African-headed companies and the first African-born woman to hold a seat in the Canadian Parliament.

"We are all African immigrants in the diaspora," Fabian says. "Standing on the same platform as these people was very humbling."

For Krystaal, life comes down to two simple priorities: God and family. Their primary focus is knowing God better and being obedient to Him.

"We are humbled by all that God has done for us," Michel says, "and we love the fact that He has called us to this ministry of music. We are committed to serving Him, no matter what."

When it comes to family, the brothers say George continues to have a strong connection with Krystaal in terms of prayer support and in the role of counsellor. Philomene has become the mother of the Lwamba family in Canada.

"Our lives are not defined by how much money we make, but by who is behind us, who lends us a shoulder to lean on when we get home," Fabian says. "It is important for people to know that we are not just three guys by ourselves. We are backed up by a wonderful family and lots of love. Love is what fires Krystaal in all that we do around the world."

The Lwamba brothers have come a long way from the desperate circumstances of the refugee camp and the crippling sense of vulnerability and anxiety that goes hand in hand with being an unwanted refugee. Such emotions are not easily forgotten. Just how deeply they are engrained became evident the first time the three stepped foot on African soil again after enjoying the freedom and security of Canada.

They were on their way to Arusha and had a brief stopover in Kenya. "I had the sense I was going back to the same situation I left," Fabian says. "I felt terribly insecure and uneasy. I was glad the stop was only for a few hours."

On the way back from Tanzania, however, the brothers spent a full day in Nairobi. They spent the night at the YMCA Hotel. It was only a stone's throw from the police station that held many terrifying memories for all three of them.

Around 8 a.m. the next morning, Fabian and Aliston went for a walk. They were gone for no more than 15 minutes, but by the time they got back to the hotel, both were drenched with nervous perspiration. Fabian recognized his paralyzing fear as a carryover from his days as an alien and refugee.

He reminded himself that things were different now. He was a Canadian citizen with a valid Canadian passport. He said to Aliston, "We have nothing to fear. We have the right to walk down these streets. We have passports."

"When we were refugees living in Nairobi, the police loved to harass us," Aliston puts in. "It seemed as if they could smell a refugee. If you tried to run away, they chased you until they caught you. If you didn't have the proper documents, they could arrest you and put you in jail. Now they call us 'Sir.'"

The sight of armed police on the streets of Nairobi no longer holds any threat for the brothers. Possessing Canadian citizenship and passports gives them confidence and boldness. It also impacts the way they handle the inevitable encounters with former Mobutu supporters, who like themselves, now live in exile outside of Zaire.

"We have met Mobutu's people in Montréal, the US, and especially in Belgium," Aliston says. "In Belgium, you find many people from both sides— the oppressors and the oppressed. In one church we visited, the pastor was welcoming a leader from Congo who had come to talk to the expatriate Congolese. This man got up on the platform and boasted, 'I worked for The Man.' Many in the congregation clapped; others wanted to kill him. The tensions are still very strong. Mobutu supporters are still out there. They still support that system and that psychology."

On a concert tour to Atlanta, the Lwambas were slightly disconcerted to recognize one of Mobutu's top military generals in the audience.

"He came to our concert," Fabian says, "and when we shared our testimony, he was overcome with guilt and began weeping. He spoke to us afterward, but he didn't say much—just that he was in exile like us. He left Zaire when Mobutu went into exile."

"These people have no power or influence over us," Michel says. "The world has changed for us. On a political level, we know our rights and our right to freedom of speech. We can speak out about what we think is right or wrong. On a spiritual level, we are bold to share our testimony because of what God has done for us and what He has called us to.

"We have a sense of freedom and belonging. What a contrast to the way we used to live! We recognize that we are privileged, and all because of God's grace. Every time we encounter someone from the camps or from our former life, it reminds us of where we've been, how far we have come, and with God's help, how far we can go."

Epilogue on Zaire

BY THE MID-1990S, MOBUTU SESE SEKO KUKU NGBENDU WA ZA BANGA, "THE all-powerful warrior who goes from conquest to conquest leaving fire in his wake" was noticeably absent in Zaire. He was failing rapidly from prostate cancer.

In his absence, a new rebel movement arose, seemingly out of nowhere, in the eastern part of the country near Kivu. In November of 1996, when Mobutu was abroad for medical treatment, Tutsis seized control of the area bordering Rwanda. Their leader was Laurent-Désiré Kabila, supported by the Tutsi governments of Rwanda, Burundi and Uganda.

In a mere six months, the anti-Mobutu forces had raced across the country and taken the capital of Kinshasa, putting to flight Mobutu's son Kongulu, captain of the dreaded DSP which was responsible for the Lubumbashi massacre. Kongulu Mobutu later died of AIDS in exile.

Laurent-Désiré Kabila installed himself as president and immediately renamed the country Democratic Republic of Congo (DR Congo).

Ravaged by cancer and too weak to put up a resistance, Mobutu Sese Seko fled to temporary exile in Togo, though he lived mostly in Rabat, Morocco. He died in exile in Morocco on September 7, 1997, and is buried in Rabat in a Christian cemetery known as "Pax."

Kabila's tenure as leader of Congo was fraught with turmoil. A rift between himself and his former allies sparked a new rebellion that was backed by

Rwanda and Uganda. Angola, Namibia and Zimbabwe sided with Kabila and the country of Congo became one vast battlefield. The International Rescue Committee, a New York-based refugee agency, estimates the conflict killed as many as 2.5 million people.

In 2001, Laurent Kabila was shot and fatally wounded by his own bodyguard and his 30-year-old son Joseph Kabila was sworn in as president.

Several democratic elections have been attempted in Congo, including one in October of 2006 in which Mobutu's son from his second marriage, François Joseph Mobutu Nzanga Ngangawe, declared himself a candidate. He was unsuccessful. Joseph Kabila became Congo's first freely elected head of state in 40 years.

Castle Quay Books